A
Separate
Circle

A Separate Circle

Jewish Life in Knoxville, Tennessee

Wendy Lowe Besmann

THE UNIVERSITY OF TENNESSEE PRESS / KNOXVILLE

The paper used in this book meets the minimum requirements of ANSI/
NISO Z39.48-1992 (R 1997) (Permanence of Paper). The binding
materials have been chosen for strength and durability.

Library of Congress Cataloging-in-Publication Data

Besmann, Wendy Lowe, 1954–
A separate circle : Jewish life in Knoxville, Tennessee /
    Wendy Lowe Besmann.
    p. cm.
Includes bibliographical references and index.
ISBN 1-57233-124-0 (cl.: alk. paper)
ISBN 1-57233-125-9 (pbk.: alk. paper)
1. Jews—Tennessee—Knoxville—History.
2. Jews—Tennessee—Knoxville—Social life and customs.
3. Judaism—Tennessee—Knoxville—History.
4. Knoxville (Tenn.)—Ethnic relations. I. Title.
F444.K7 B47 2001
976.8'85004924—dc21   00-011709

This book is dedicated with love to my husband, Ted
(who was disappointed that I wouldn't use his favorite
title idea, Aren't Jew a Vol)*, as well as to my daughter,*
Anna, my son, David, and my mother-in-law, Greta.
All four Besmanns read various parts of the manuscript,
made useful comments, and suffered through my lengthy
efforts with as much patience as they could muster.

Contents

$\mathcal{I}$llustrations

Acknowledgments

More than one hundred individuals who live or once lived in the Knoxville–Morristown–Oak Ridge area contributed their stories to this book. Many graciously agreed to be interviewed on multiple occasions and searched their personal files for useful material. I am very grateful to all those who participated.

The Knoxville Jewish Federation (KJF) supported this research with a substantial grant from its Fund for Jewish Continuity. KJF's Archives of the Jewish Community of Knoxville and East Tennessee provided a large number of the photographs included in these pages in addition to many useful documents. Generous grants were also provided by the Southern Jewish Historical Society as well as by Barbara Winick Bernstein and Bernard E. Bernstein. I wish to express my bottomless gratitude to Barbara, who served as coach, critic, angel, and enthusiastic coworker on so many aspects of this project. It would have been nearly impossible to reconstruct the story of Knoxville's Jews if she had not initiated a project during the 1980s which produced oral histories of prominent local Jewish citizens, many of whom were long deceased by the time I began my research. Her enormous historical files, filled with family pictures, correspondence, and the gossipy accounts of everyday events, were a primary source of information for me. Bernie Bernstein also reviewed large portions of the material and helped correct many errors.

Special thanks are also due my good friends Mary Linda and Arnold Schwarzbart, who not only contributed their own family stories but also read the complete manuscript at various stages. They clued me in or straightened me out on everything from the music played at bar mitzvah parties in the 1950s to the correct transliteration of Yiddish phrases. Mary Linda served as a peer reviewer for University of Tennessee Press at the final manuscript stage and has been unstinting with her encouragement. I am especially grateful to Mary Linda for providing minutes of early Hadassah chapter meetings and to Lee Miller, who preserved an archive of Hadassah directories. Both were rich sources of information.

Knoxville attorney Scott Hahn was an endless font of stories, photographs, documents, and juicy gossip from long ago. Whenever I encountered him during the several years it took to produce this book, he always questioned me about the project and usually had a new source to suggest.

At several points in this project, I received valuable assistance from Jewish historians and Judaic Studies scholars. Many thanks to Dr. Gilya Gerda Schmidt, who holds the chair of Judaic Studies at University of Tennessee. She recommended me as an author for this book to University of Tennessee Press and frequently offered advice on the publication process. Dr. Leonard Dinnerstein, author of numerous works on Jewish history and director of University of Arizona's Judaic Studies program, read the entire manuscript twice as the academic reviewer for University of Tennessee Press. He urged me to place the story of Knoxville's Jews in a broader national and regional context, then provided many useful suggestions for doing so. Advice, encouragement, and reading lists were also provided at important junctures by the editor of the journal *Southern Jewish History*, Dr. Mark Bauman of Atlanta Metropolitan College, and by Deborah Weiner at University of West Virginia. Many thanks to historian Hollace Weiner in Fort Worth, Texas; Dr. Mark Greenberg of the Museum of the Southern Jewish Experience; and Dr. Leonard Rogoff, research historian at Rosenzweig Museum and Jewish Heritage Foundation of North Carolina, for advice and perspective. I am indebted to Ann Silverstein at the Beth Ahabah Museum and Archives in Richmond, Virginia, for locating important information about early Knoxville

Jewish history in her own files. The work of local historian and journalist Jack Neely, as well as his many excellent tips, proved invaluable. Original inspiration for this work was a long article I wrote for *MetroPulse*, for which assignment I wish to thank editor Joe Sullivan and the *MetroPulse* staff.

Here in Knoxville, community members Richard Licht, David Levy, Genevieve Kramer, Mel Sturm, Myra Corkland Weinstein, and Harold Winston were particularly generous in sharing their own prodigious research into family history. Local attorney and genealogist Nicole Russler also gave me valuable insights into Jewish immigration history and the many curious ways that Eastern European Jewish families got their American surnames.

Many thanks to the following individuals, who were interviewed or otherwise provided information and photographic material for this book: Martin Abrams, Paul Agron, Nancy and Jeffrey Becker, Joe and Helen Billig, Serkie Billig, Mirian Reich Blumberg, Pam Branton, Zelmore and Jamie Brody, Adam Brown, Elaine Brown, Mary Brown, Dr. Michael Burnett, Marilyn Burnett, Milton Carey, Arnold Cohen, Gert Cohen, Rody and Neil Cohen, Gertrude Danziger, Dr. Harold and Joyce Diftler, Trudy Dreyer, Dr. Henry and Claudia Fribourg, Joseph and Marion Goodstein, Dora Green, Anne Greenbaum, Rabbi Mark Greenspan, Tommy Hahn, Eileen Handler, Shelley Hanford, Peggy Leibowitz Hedrick, Herb and Myra Hoffman, Marian Jay, Sybil Joffe, Jack Kessler, Mira Kimmelman, Mildred Landay, Bella Leeds, Harold and Sylvia Leibowitz, Mary Beth Leibowitz, Larry Leibowitz, Rabbi Shlomo Levine, Gilbert Levison, Harvey and Marilyn Liberman, Mary and Rose Kate Lippner, Harold Markman, Harry and Ursula Marx, Muriel Marvet, Nora and Patrick Messing, Anita Miller, Lee Miller, Melissa Miller, Sarah Miller, Drs. Howard and Marilyn Pollio, Marilyn Presser, Rabbi Victor Rashkovsky, Rabbi Geela Rayzel Raphael, Simcha Raphael, Mitchell and Natalie Robinson, Pace, Karen, Eli and Asher Robinson, Alexandra Rosen, Stephen Rosen, Esther Rosen, Gene Rosenberg, Maurice Schwarzenberg, Rabbi Beth L. Schwartz, Selma Shapiro, Harold and Addie Shersky, Fran Silver, Sylvia Silver, Rabbi Howard and Rona Simon, Toby Slabosky, Norbert Slovis, Fran Sturm, Melissa Sturm, Barry Winston, Becky Winston, and Rabbi

Arthur Weiner. If any names have been left off this long list (or heaven forbid, misspelled), I truly apologize. The interest and support shown by the community has been wonderful.

Finally, I am grateful for stories provided by late community members Ruth Carey, Harry Marx, Sarah Green Robinson, and Bradley Sturm. May their memories be a blessing, and may their commitment to the Jewish community be honored among us always. ∞

One

Laying Down the Stones

noxville's New Jewish Cemetery keeps a very low profile among the Gentile neighbors. Even though it has stretched across the corner of Glenn and Keith Avenues for more than a century, you won't find a listing among all the other burial grounds plotted with tiny red crosses on Knoxville street maps. Tall shrubbery and chain-link fencing provide a certain distance from the surrounding cluster of mid-century bungalows coated in pastel hues of aluminum siding. If you're new in town, you have to ask somebody for directions. On the south side of Glenn Avenue, where construction crews have been slowly widening Middlebrook Pike into an industrial highway, the street sign is sometimes missing. Watch for the narrow intersection across from a stubby little church called the Crown of Hope. Turn right and go up a block. The short, steep driveway at the cemetery's entrance is unmarked except for a small plaque in memory of Oscar Glazer, who founded the family's scrap metal business.

Once inside, the driveway cuts a broad circular path through the middle of a gently sloping square. More than just a convenience for mourners, this pathway subtly telegraphs the most basic division among Knoxville Jews. Graves for members of the Reform congregation Temple Beth El lie mostly within the central circle and to the right of the drive. Members of Heska Amuna Synagogue, the Conservative congregation, are usually buried on the left. In all other respects, the two populations seem identical. Jewish cemeteries tend toward an elegant severity, avoiding the statuary of Christian burial sites in favor of plain monuments with names, dates, and inspirational phrases carved in Hebrew or English. Here, there are only two departures from the norm: a tall obelisk to Knoxville Jewish servicemen fallen in World War II and a large mausoleum that a grieving merchant named Morris Bart commissioned after the sudden passing of his young wife in 1913. All the other tributes to a century of life and death form neat rows of polished gray granite or rust-brown marble. The only adornments are small piles of gleaming white pebbles scattered on the turf around most of the headstones. Floral arrangements—which the Jews traditionally save for joyous occasions—are rarely present in this cemetery. I can't help noticing as I climb out of my car on a sweltering day in early fall that the only spots of bright color are the tiny, red ribbons engraved on the joint headstone of Dan Goodman and David McNabb Abramson. Popular and respected attorneys, these two life partners and members of Heska Amuna Synagogue died of AIDS. On the back of the stone is carved the Hebrew word *chutzpah*. I'm told it refers to the name of Goodman's beloved dog, as well as to a general attitude toward life.

In the family plot next to Mr. Goodman lies my father-in-law, Siegfried Besmann. He and my husband's mother, Greta, both Holocaust-era refugees who settled in New York, came to share Passover with us in Knoxville a few years ago. Sigi became ill and lingered for many months in a local hospital. Though he was a stranger in this town, members of the Jewish community often came to visit him and support my mother-in-law through the various medical crises they faced together. Finally, in the hottest part of summer, Sigi passed away and was buried in Knoxville, very far from his own Jewish roots. A small committee of Synagogue members served as *hevra kadisha*, the sacred society that washes and prepares a Jew for burial with precise rituals and ancient prayers. Others volunteered to be the *shomrim*, the sacred guardians who take turns reading psalms beside the coffin throughout the night until the time comes for the funeral. Still others were his pallbearers, and others of the *chesed* committee came to bring us the traditional "meal of condolence" when we returned from the cemetery. One placed a pitcher of water by our front door so that we might ritually wash away the dust of the cemetery from our hands and reenter the household of the living. Then we were ushered to the dining table to eat a light lunch that included hard-boiled eggs, which symbolize new life. During the *shiva*, the seven days of mourning, people came to visit my husband and his mother, bringing little gifts of food and encouraging us to speak of Sigi. Other Synagogue members formed a daily *minyan*, the gathering of at least ten adults that is required for saying Kaddish, the ancient memorial prayer that mourners recite daily during this time. Such acts, done for the dead and the living, are called *gemilut chasadim*—deeds of loving kindness. Yet they are also considered to be among the most ordinary responsibilities that one Jew owes to any other. In the midst of grief these small duties are intended to connect us to one another within the great silken chain of our tradition.

Sigi was a pious man who believed deeply in that chain. I think he would be pleased to be cared for by these strangers who weren't strangers because they were fellow Jews. I like to think he would also be pleased that I have come to his resting place on this particular day in early fall to perform another simple, ancient ritual that binds one generation to the next. I've come to do what Jews do when visiting a cemetery, particularly during the holy days between Rosh Hoshana and Yom Kippur. I have come to lay a stone.

Jewish time is counted by a lunar calendar that runs from autumn to autumn. We are now in the first month, Tishrei, which begins with the observance of Rosh Hoshana, the New Year. In this season, even Jews who rarely attend services show up in such great numbers that until recently the Synagogue assigned tickets to paid-up members and stopped others at the door with reminders of the need to share the financial burden of maintaining a Jewish community. The most prominent part of the Rosh Hoshana service is the blowing of the *shofar*. This is a ritual ram's horn whose raw, shrill blast is a kind of primal connection to the tribes who called each other from ancient hilltops in Judaea. Ten days later comes Yom Kippur, the Day of Atonement, when an equally large crowd gathers to fast and pray for the forgiveness of sins until the all-day service ends with a final blowing of the shofar. Together these two holidays form the High Holy Days, the first in a rich cycle of shared celebration that moves any Jewish community from season to season and through the major passages of life.

Last week was Rosh Hoshana. Like most parents of school-age children, my own time was split between the main sanctuary—where solemn prayers were being chanted from morning through mid-afternoon—and the various classrooms where fractious youngsters were kept entertained with card games and puzzles. The halls between buzzed with people lingering on their way in and out of the sanctuary to exchange New Year's greetings. If the face seemed familiar but the name didn't come, it was enough to nod, pat a back or touch an arm, and murmur *"shana tova"* or *"gut yontiff."* These phrases are Americanized shorthand for the traditional Hebrew and Yiddish greetings of the season: *L'shana tova tikateyvu* ("may you be inscribed and sealed [in the Book of Life] for a good year") and *gut yom tov* ("good holiday"). By midday the lobby is always densely crowded with people casually taking a break from the long services, shushed intermittently by ushers who are schmoozing as much as the crowd they monitor— "L'shana tova, gut yontiff. How're you? Don't you look nice. Your children are getting so tall! So, how was your summer? Your mother, she's well?" No doubt the same conversation is repeated a few hundred times in this room and another few hundred times in the lobby of Temple Beth El, located half a mile away. Peering into the Heska Amuna library, I see the big, shabby chairs are filled as usual with lounging teenagers, some of them Temple members who have strolled along Kingston Pike to visit with their friends at the Synagogue. They don't know it, but this teenage tradition goes back to the early decades of the century, when the two tiny Knoxville congregations stood at a cozy distance from one another in the downtown neighborhood where most Jews lived and worked. The New Year is a kind of Jewish family reunion, and after the service most people will regroup for genial family luncheons. My husband and I have no family here, but for many years we have been invited for Rosh Hoshana lunch at the home of Barbara Winick Bernstein, whose grandfather was the Synagogue's first rabbi more than a hundred years ago.

Barbara Bernstein, an amateur historian of considerable skill, has collected cabinets full of documents, photos, taped interviews, and letters related to early Knoxville Jewish history. She and her sister Muriel Winick Marvet come from a long line of ardent diarists. Their family members not only produced great volumes of journal notes and correspondence but also cared enough to save them for posterity. That same Rosh Hoshana afternoon, Barbara showed me a letter written by her father, Ben Winick, then a young attorney who volunteered to report on the famous Scopes trial in Dayton, Tennessee, for the *Daily Forward*, a Yiddish newspaper. "Some of the biggest scientists in the world are here testifying relative to evolution, and to listen to them is an education in itself," the son of the Orthodox rabbi wrote to his future wife, Clara Katz, the daughter of a prominent Temple family. "From the looks of things, this trial is going down in history."

My husband and I are newcomers to this town, washed in on a wavelet of Jewish professionals who settled around Knoxville during the mid-1970s. I come from people who moved a lot, rarely bothering to record much family history, not even those dazzling moments when a personal trajectory will suddenly intersect the march of great events. Perhaps that is why I am so fascinated by the sense of history and rootedness I find in this small, obscure corner of world Jewry. After twenty-some years in the East Tennessee Jewish community, I am slowly grafting on my own roots. When Sigi died, we followed the usual custom of reserving an entire family plot. That polished marble headstone engraved with the name Besmann is a tangible reminder to me that—barring some new quirk of fate—my own name will someday be listed among all the others in this burial ground. Some might consider this a morbid thought, but I find it strangely comforting.

Of course, the New Year is a propitious moment for a Jew to think about her place in history. From the start of Rosh Hoshana through Yom Kippur stretch the ten days of *teshuva*, or repentance. By tradition, these ten days are the time when the Book of Life is open but not sealed, when our actions have not yet accumulated the consequences that will befall us in the coming year. The sages taught that one must live carefully during this time, reevaluate priorities, assess where one has been and where one is going. That sense of settling up all moral accounts probably led to the centuries-old custom of going to a relative's burial place during this ten days. Memorial services will be held here before Yom Kippur, but some, like me, drop by for a more informal visit. In addition to a short prayer, the main custom is to pick up a small, unremarkable stone from the ground and lay it atop the grave marker. The stones lie there until wind or weather tumble them down again. Nobody knows exactly why the custom took this form or why it remains so entrenched in tradition. Some say it hearkens back to the cairns of stone under which the Israelites buried their dead during the forty years of desert wandering. The scholar Rabbi David Wolpe notes that in ancient times a shepherd counted his sheep at the beginning of the day by carrying the corresponding number of stones, and these were used to ascertain that the same number of sheep returned at night. Therefore, the stones may symbolize how precious each soul is to God, who "counts" each person in the world.

Never mind. Laying a stone is something a Jew does, a mark of respect for the changing of seasons and the passing of generations, a ritual like so many other Jewish rituals that link us together in a journey through time. I pick up one of the small, white pebbles from the ground and place it gently atop the gray marble on Sigi's grave.

On a fine Sunday morning in the spring of 1998, I got a short tour of this place from Scott Hahn, longtime chairman of the Cemetery Committee for Heska Amuna Synagogue. His counterpart at the Temple is University of Tennessee professor Dr. Henry Fribourg, who kindly supplied me with a detailed list of Temple burials over the past century. As with so many practical matters in this town, the Temple and Synagogue tend to zealously guard their separate bits of turf.

Scott Hahn is a Knoxville lawyer whose great grandfather was a prominent local politician. Now in his late thirties, Scott is just old enough to remember a time when the Jewish community was a cousins club of merchant families linked by ties of blood, marriage, social relationships, and business affairs. That morning, we counted eight different family names to which he is directly related. Later, I trailed behind him on a circuitous journey between the gravestones, scribbling furiously in my notebook as he told me a dozen or so tales of sensational deaths. There was the early-morning car explosion linked to rumors of shadowy business deals. There was the prominent married businessman who drowned on a pleasure boat in the company of his mistress, setting off a great flurry in the local press. Perhaps most unsettling of all was the grisly death of a wealthy jeweler's wife, still unsolved after thirty years. She was found in her living room, stabbed many times and nearly scalped. A rented policeman's uniform was found in the bushes outside her Sequoyah Hills door, and local Jews still whisper their suspicions. Such details are intriguing bits of scarlet scandal in the tapestry of a small community, woven against a sturdy fabric of a thousand much more ordinary tales about getting by, building up, falling apart, and starting over.

The history of the East Tennessee Jewish community is sealed within these ordinary tales and buried in this ground. Here beneath these markers lie the immigrant peddlers who ventured into primitive farm settlements with a wagonload of goods and a few words of broken English. Here lie the people who ran grocery stores and pawnshops, the people who sold dresses and shoes and auto parts and beauty supplies. Over here is the stone of a quiet record-store owner who helped make Elvis a star; over there is the stone of a man with political connections who (local legend insists) told FDR what to call the New Deal. Here, too, lie the people who served on committees, who argued over bylaws, who pestered their friends for donations to the building fund. Here lie the belles of Purim Balls at the old Jewish Community Center on Vine Street. Here lie the basketball heroes who dashed down the court of the old Center gym with Stars of David blazoned on their jerseys. Here lie the postwar parents who gathered for coffee at Harold's Deli on Gay Street while their kids learned at the Center's joint Sunday school. Here lie the struggling Jewish shopkeepers who raised their sons and daughters to be affluent Jewish professionals. Here lie the echoes of a hundred bitter family feuds, a thousand quiet acts of generosity, and the day-to-day minutiae that can make a community hang together for more than 135 years.

In nineteenth-century America, organized life in a Jewish community most often started with a cemetery. Jewish pioneers were practical sorts who spared little time for religious ritual, but death was another matter entirely. Then, as now, the two most widely practiced rites were circumcision of male babies on the eighth day after birth and Jewish burial. Wherever a small group of Jews put down roots, the need for a cemetery would soon be discussed. Next would come a move to collect funds for the sick and indigent—for the tradition of being responsible for the physical welfare of fellow Jews is deeply ingrained in the culture. The next item on the communal agenda was to start a religious school for the children. Last on the list was a formal house of worship to replace the informal *minyan*, or prayer group, composed of at least ten adult men. First they dealt with life and death, then health and prosperity, then learning and prayer. This practical sequence of priorities was taking shape in thousands of small Jewish communities across the American frontier by the fall of 1860, when the heads of a few Knoxville Jewish households met to arrange the first cemetery.

The exact starting point of their story is unclear. No one is sure when the first Jews arrived in East Tennessee, though a curious near miss is recorded in the early 1700s. It seems that Scottish adventurer Sir Alexander Cuming hatched a moneymaking scheme to colonize 300,000 European Jewish families between 1740 and 1750 in the Cherokee lands that are now part of East Tennessee. Apparently, he had explored that wilderness in 1730 and prevailed on the natives to sign a peace treaty with the British. Sir Alexander's goal was personal and government profit. The idea was for immigrating Jews to pay off $400 million of the British debt and eventually join the native Indians in a mass conversion to Christianity. Cuming is said to have shopped the idea around to some eminent London Jews, whose reaction is unknown. His plan was eventually rejected by the government of George II, and thus East Tennessee missed the opportunity to become the new Jewish homeland.

The first small wave of Jewish settlers were Sephardim, whose lineage came from the once wealthy and sophisticated Jewish communities of Spain and Portugal. Over centuries of exile, the world's Jewish population had split into two major groups whose religious beliefs stayed the same while their culture, rituals, ethnic foods, and everyday spoken language diverged to reflect very different environments. The Sephardim lived in the Muslim lands of the Mediterranean, North Africa, Spain, and Portugal, while the Ashkenazim settled primarily in Christian Germany and Eastern Europe. While the

Ashkenazim were often confined to ghettos and restricted economically, the Sephardim mingled much more freely in Muslim society and often rose to positions of prominence. The Sephardic Golden Age came to an end in 1492, after Catholic kings wrested Spain and Portugal from the Moors and began to expel, murder, and forcibly convert the Jewish population. Remnants of this community gradually drifted to New World colonies in South America and the Caribbean, while a small group showed up in what later became New York during the 1650s.

As new colonies developed, enterprising Sephardic Jews appeared in New Orleans and Charleston, making their way through the frontier south first as traveling peddlers, then as shopkeepers and landowners. By the time of the American Revolution, a few may have penetrated as far as the Tennessee River to trade with the Indians. A man named Solomon D. Jacobs is listed as mayor of Knoxville in 1835. The late Dr. Jacob Marcus, venerable archivist for Hebrew Union College, reportedly found traces of a "Rabbi" Abraham Ben Jaddai living in Knoxville prior to 1840. Ben Jaddai is even said to have authored a book in defense of Judaism. A certain Levi Israel also shows up in the 1840 census for Knox County but never reappears.

A larger wave of Ashkenazic Jewish immigrants came to the South from the French-German province of Alsace-Lorraine in the 1840s, after Germany regained territory once captured by Napoleon. Jews who had briefly enjoyed the status of emancipated citizens under Napoleonic rule had now fallen back under the more repressive political and economic constraints imposed by the Germans. Meanwhile, German revolutionary upheavals and an economic slump in the region encouraged many Bavarian, Austrian, and Hungarian Jews to emigrate. A steady trickle began to arrive at southern ports such as New Orleans and Galveston. Many became peddlers, carving out sales territory through the river towns along the Mississippi and the frontier areas radiating around them. Some went north and west, but more settled in the southern states. By the early 1850s, Jewish congregations had formed in Memphis and Nashville, which still maintain the state's largest Jewish populations.

A handful of Alsatian or German Jewish names—Dreyfous, Joseph, Schwab, and several families of Lyons—appear in Knoxville's first city directory, published in 1859, when the town had fewer than three thousand inhabitants. One ran a small grocery, one was a tailor, and another was an auctioneer. During the late 1850s a clothier named Solomon Lyons, who had lately come down from Keokuk, Iowa, formed Lyons & Sherer, which advertised itself as "Manufacturers of Bonnets and Mantillas, dealers in Dry Goods, Boots & Shoes." At some point a new partner named Joseph Mayer came on the scene, and the two men purchased a small plot of land, 50 feet by 120 feet, just east of downtown in a section called Shieldstown (now the corner of Winona and Linden Streets).

By the fall of 1861, war between the states seemed inevitable. Solomon Lyons invited Knoxville's seven Jewish families to a meeting in his home and offered the use of his company's plot as a burial ground. The land was first put to use two years later when Knoxville liquor merchant Abraham Schwab brought home the body of his eighteen-year-old son, Joseph, who had died of typhoid fever while serving with the Confederate army in Virginia. (Abraham Schwab's daughter Cecilia was also the first Jewish bride to be married in Knoxville. City records show that for some unknown reason she was married to her husband, Morris Saltzkotler, once by a justice of the peace in 1857 and again by another justice of the peace in 1860.) Several other burials were made in 1862–63, including another Confederate soldier named Isaac Stern.

My friend Shelley Hanford recently showed me a large mounted copy of a mid-nineteenth-century Knoxville street map. It now sits in the kindergarten classroom at Temple Beth El. On a plastic overlay sheet, some unknown Temple historian has neatly plotted the business and home addresses of Jewish families listed in the 1859 and 1869 city directories. The first thing I noticed is that everyone lived and worked in a ten-block radius bordered to the north and east by Temperance and Vine Streets, both of which vanished completely during urban renewal a century later. The second thing I noticed is that most of the six family names listed in 1859 are no longer present among the dozen or so family names that appear ten years later. Southern Jews were transient in the first years after the war. Knoxville, judged a rich prize of war because its natural deposits of saltpeter were vital to making gunpowder, had been the site of bloody clashes between the two armies. East Tennessee went for the Union, but Knoxville itself was a welter of divided opinion.

The Jews of Knoxville, like Jews all over America, mostly chose sides according to their own regional loyalties. At the start of the Civil War, almost as many Jews lived in the South as in the North. They served in both armies as foot soldiers and officers. One such officer was General Louis A. Gratz, a German immigrant who was peddling in Pittstown, Pennsylvania, when he joined the Union army. He wrote back to his family in Germany, "My dear ones, I beg with all my heart not to be angry because I have gone to war—and should it be my destiny to lose my life, well I will have sacrificed it for a cause to which I am attached with all my heart, that is the liberation of the United States." Gratz rose through the ranks from first lieutenant to major to eventually become acting assistant adjutant general for the Third Division of the 23d Army Corps. When he was mustered out in Tennessee in 1865, he chose to settle in Knoxville and gain admittance to the Tennessee Bar. Though he also opened a grocery downtown on Crozier Street, Gratz seems to have practiced successfully as a lawyer, serving twice as Knoxville City attorney. He married the socially prominent Elizabeth Bearden, whose father was mayor of Knoxville and whose family lent its name to what is now an affluent section of west Knoxville. Starting in the early 1890s, Gratz served four terms as mayor of north Knoxville, where Gratz Street is named after him. Though he made no secret of his heritage, he apparently didn't identify with the tiny Jewish congregation, and he followed his wife's family to the First Presbyterian Church. Recently our local newspaper ran the obituary of his granddaughter Margaret Ernest, who was born on Gratz Street near the stroke of midnight on January 1, 1900, and died at the ripe old age of ninety-nine. A pillar of the church and the city's toniest charities, this granddaughter of a German Jew helped organize the first Knoxville chapters of the Colonial Dames of America and the Daughters of the American Revolution. (As the journalist Harry Golden—who profiled Louis Gratz in his book *Jews in American History*—was famous for saying, "Only in America!")

Apparently, some German Jews chose to join the Confederacy because their youthful contact with republican struggles in Germany left them sympathetic to the Southerner's cry for autonomy. One such advocate of states' rights was Bavarian immigrant Emanuel Samuel, listed in the 1869 directory as president of the Knoxville Hebrew Benevolent Society. His descendant Richard Licht, who still lives in Knoxville and presides over the family's century-old condiment company, relates the family story that Emanuel had originally settled in Pennsylvania but was forced to escape from that state under a loaded wagon because his Confederate sympathies riled the neighbors. (Richard Licht and his cousin David Levy, who owns Beltone Hearing Aid Center in Knoxville, head the only two remaining families descended from the original signers of the Hebrew Benevolent Association constitution. Levy is descended from Samuel Samuels, brother and business partner of Emanuel. His son Brian Adam, a University of Tennessee student, is the sixth generation of the family to live in Knoxville.)

Emanuel's grandson Milton Levy, a commercial artist, supplied a few details on his ancestor in a letter he wrote for the Temple's one hundredth anniversary in 1964. He reports that Emanuel "served in the cavalry on the Confederate side, having his own horse, pistol and blanket; he fought at the battle of Fort Sanders and other battles in Tennessee as far west as Shiloh." He seems to have left off soldiering for a peddler's life, making frequent horseback trips on the "buckboard" road between Knoxville and Sevierville. If he was thirsty, he would stash his silver flask behind a tree with a dollar stuck beneath it and continue up into the mountains to buy ginseng roots from the locals. On his return trip, he would find the dollar gone and the container filled with moonshine whiskey. All in all, Knoxville seemed like a good place to settle. Before the war's end, Emanuel and his brother Samuel opened a dry goods store off Church Street. The family reports they "sold blankets to both sides."

In fact, many Jewish merchants served as contractors who provided goods to the armies. Others were sutlers who sold the troops luxuries such as coffee, sugar, and tobacco. In the last years of war, some of these merchants were undoubtedly engaged in the lucrative smuggling trade. The temptation to dabble in selling the spoils of war was so great that at one point many Union officers were grossly neglecting their war duties to pad their own personal fortunes. The

Emanuel Samuel *(center, third from left)*, a signatory to the Knoxville Hebrew Benevolent Association constitution and president of Temple Beth El, is pictured with his large family in this portrait taken near the turn of the century. His great-grandson Richard Licht still lives in Knoxville. Courtesy of Richard Licht.

Northern press began to publish accounts of smuggling that pointedly blamed Jews for the mess. Against this backdrop of suspicion, Tennessee became the site of a bizarre episode in Civil War history, an attempt by General Ulysses S. Grant to crack down on illegal smuggling by emptying the territory of all Jews.

The general was under extreme pressure to halt the speculators who were selling captured warehouses of cotton to the North in exchange for the gold so desperately needed by the cash-poor Confederate army. One of the speculators was Grant's own father, Jesse, who had a Jewish business partner. Staff members also reported that some of the most successful speculators among his own civilian bureaucracy were Jews. On December 17, 1862, the general impetuously issued General Orders Number 11, which began, "The Jews, as a class, violating every regulation of trade, are hereby expelled." Within twenty-four hours, all Jews were to leave the territory that now includes most of Kentucky and Tennessee as far east as the Holston River. Dozens of families had to pack up and leave. "He was looking for a scapegoat on which to vent his pent-up anger and frustration," writes Grant biographer Geoffrey Perret. "Not for the first time in history Jews fit the bill."

The order was quite unenforceable, since Grant obviously couldn't expel Jewish soldiers serving in his own regiments or the many Jewish contractors who sold basic supplies to his armies. Up north, Jewish leaders quietly intervened with President Abraham Lincoln, who revoked the order two weeks after it was issued. Grant later admitted he had no right to act against an entire religious group and said, "The order was made and sent out without any reflection." This was the only wartime decree against an ethnic or religious group ever issued by the American government until the internment of Japanese American citizens during World War II. (Ironically, President Ulysses S. Grant would later become the first American head of state to take action on behalf of oppressed Jews. In 1869 he intervened with Tsarist authorities to effectively halt the planned expulsion of twenty thousand Jews from an area in southwest Russia.)

Knoxville lay on the border of the zone affected by Grant's expulsion order, and there is no record that any of its Jewish families were displaced. Still, there was little time for community building in the tumult of war and Reconstruction. The cemetery arrangement wasn't formalized until August of 1864. Mayer & Lyons conveyed the land (for one dollar) to the Knoxville Hebrew Benevolent Association in a document signed by Solomon Lyons and the brace of newcomers who settled in Knoxville just after the war: D. March, Edward Stern, Moses Stern, Joseph Lyons, Louis David, Joseph David, Isaac Hooman, Sampson Hirsch, Isadore Fishel, J. Solomon, A. Gosdorfer, G. Gottlieb, Samuel Guggenheim, Jacob Spiesburger, B. W. Wise, David Marks, M. Heart, and Frank Heart. The new association didn't receive its formal charter from the reconstructed State of Tennessee until March 3, 1868, and delayed signing a constitution until the summer of 1869. At this point, its stated purpose was to "provide services in the Ashkenazi (German) form, provide a Jewish cemetery, and to collect funds for indigent and distressed Jews." The city directory for that year indicates worship services were held the first Sunday of each month in the home of Victor Burger, who ran a dry goods store near the Deaf and Dumb Asylum off Vine Street (later Old City Hall). Within a few decades, this neighborhood would become the heart of Jewish Knoxville.

A footnote on the way to community: The original cemetery proved troublesome. Several burials were mistakenly made on adjoining land owned by Peter Staub, a Swiss businessman who operated a popular theater on Gay Street. The Jewish community acquired the land from Staub but couldn't find a way to keep this low-lying ground from flooding after every big rain. Near the turn of the century, funds were collected to purchase the New Jewish Cemetery off Middlebrook Pike, then a quiet country lane at the western edge of the city. Until the 1970s, some of the old families continued to use the original site near downtown, now located in a neighborhood of shabby houses and industrial offices. The Knoxville Jewish community no longer includes any living descendants of the forty people buried here, but the small gated square is still carefully maintained.

Meanwhile, the tiny circle of German *Juden* was about to change dramatically. The *Yidden* were coming from Eastern Europe, and the impact of their arrival would be felt all over the South. ∾

Two

Famous Sons

M y favorite pizza joint in Knoxville is downtown on Market Square, a rather pretty outdoor mall with one good restaurant surrounded by a lot of vacant storefronts. Despite numerous tries, nobody has quite figured out how to remake the historic square into one of those stroll-about-dining-browsing-let's-do-coffee areas that draw so many customers in other cities.

In a collection of old postcards called *Knoxville, Tennessee*, I saw pictures of Market Square in its glory days five or six decades ago, when it was crammed full of businesses clustered around the big indoor Market House. Cars and delivery trucks were shoehorned into tight diagonal lanes between the surrounding rim of stores and the barnlike structure at the center. Inside, the old Market House was dim and eternally pungent with its mixture of fruits, vegetables, flowers, great slabs of meat hung from hooks in the ceiling, and whole fish cooling on broad cakes of ice. Much of Knoxville's fresh food was sold here, and around the square you could buy everything from shoes and men's suits to hardware and country music. The beginning of the end was in late 1959, when the teenaged son of a local merchant reportedly sneaked up in the loft to smoke a cigarette. The whole place burned down. Nobody ever got around to rebuilding the structure, especially since people and businesses were already disappearing west into the new suburbs.

Eventually, TVA's Twin Towers rose just north of the site, and downtown gradually became repopulated with lawyers, bankers, and

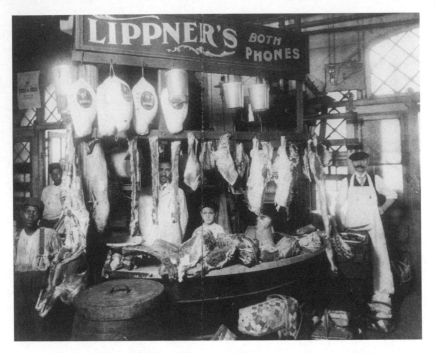

Lippner's Meat Market, run by two Lippner brothers in the old Market House. In the early days, it included kosher and nonkosher sides. Courtesy of Knoxville Jewish Federation.

office workers. Now Market Square is pretty quiet on a weekday morning, except for some old farmers selling vegetables and dusty jars of pickled stuff. Chairs are still up on tables inside The Tomato Head Cafe, and the young staff is playing rock music to suit themselves while they cook the fragrant pizza dough and straighten up all the flyers for struggling/alternative entertainment experiences. Meanwhile, they serve excellent coffee and bagels, so this is where I arranged to meet Jack Neely, who writes the "Secret History" column for *MetroPulse*. The weekly newspaper's offices are a few steps away in the old Arnstein Building at Market and Union. Having crammed so many gratuitous plugs into one paragraph, I might as well add that Jack Neely's columns have been collected in two very entertaining volumes called *Knoxville's Secret History*. The first volume contains several good stories about local Jews, some of which appear in this book. (No remuneration was received for this unqualified endorsement, but Jack did insist on buying the latte that morning.)

More to the point, Jack also reminded me about a small brass plaque at Gay Street and Cumberland on the original nineteenth-century site of Staub's Theater. The last line on the plaque reads, "Adolph Ochs, later publisher of the *New York Times*, was its first chief usher." The owner of that theater was Peter Staub, the Swiss immigrant whose lot adjoining the first Jewish cemetery in Shieldstown had accidentally received a few of its departed. Luckily, he was genial about selling the Jews this bit of land, and even more genial about helping the enterprising fourteen-year-old son of Julius Ochs, his onetime business partner.

Julius Ochs and his wife, Bertha Levy Ochs, lived in Knoxville briefly just before the start of the Civil War. An advertisement in the *Knoxville Register* for November 1, 1855, reads "To the ladies of Knoxville and vicinity: Mrs. Bertha Ochs and her sister Miss Fanny Levy will give lessons in Embroidery, Needlework and all other kinds of Ladies' Fancy Work, Sewing, Fine Stitching, etc. Having been educated in one of the best academies of Europe they feel confident that they will give general satisfaction. Their method is simple and easy. Terms will be liberal. Apply to Mrs. Ochs, Cumberland Street near the corner of Market."

As a teenage schoolgirl in Bavaria, the cultivated Mrs. Ochs was involved with the German revolutionary movement of 1848. When another German student protester was shot, she and several friends went out in the street to catch his blood on their handkerchiefs, which they publicly preserved as holy relics. After that, the police began to investigate young Bertha, and her family was advised to get her out of the country before serious trouble ensued. Sent to stay with an uncle in Natchez, Mississippi, she became an equally passionate supporter of states' rights. The rest of her family immigrated a few years later, and she went with them to Nashville. There she met and married Julius, another well-educated Bavarian immigrant, whose father, Lazarus Ochsenhorn, was a prosperous diamond merchant and Talmudic scholar. After immigrating in 1845 to avoid repressive anti-Jewish laws, Julius had knocked around the South in a variety of jobs, briefly teaching French at a girls' school in Mount Sterling, Kentucky.

The young couple moved to Cincinnati by the start of the Civil War, so Julius (who had served with Federal troops in the Mexican War of the 1840s) joined the 52d Ohio Volunteers as a captain in charge of drilling troops. This sat very poorly with his staunchly Confederate wife. At one point during the war, she placed a load of quinine in the bottom of her son's baby carriage and coolly attempted to cross over the Ohio River Bridge to deliver this precious medical contraband to Confederate troops on the other side. She was briefly detained, but the gallantry of the times and her marriage to a Union officer apparently saved her from punishment. One story reports that Julius Och's good friend Andrew Johnson (then vice president of the United States) intervened directly to work out a deal whereby Mrs. Ochs could avoid prison if she promised to give up smuggling for the duration. Nonetheless, when Bertha Ochs died in 1908, she was buried at her own request beneath a Confederate flag, while Julius was laid to rest beneath the Stars and Stripes. Much later, Adolph and his brother George each stubbornly claimed to have been the baby in that carriage, though it was probably George, who was younger and smaller at the time.

Julius Ochs moved his family back to Knoxville in the late 1860s, drawn like so many other immigrant Jews to the wide-open opportunities in rebuilding a shattered Southern economy. The city directory for 1876 lists him as "Justice of the Peace, Notary Public, U.S. Commissioner and Fire Insurance Agent." Though highly respected for his learning, Ochs was apparently more of a dreamer than an entrepreneur. Every one of his ventures failed, including his brief partnership with Staub. The family barely scraped by. Adolph later recalled with gratitude the kindly neighbor who cut down an old pair of her husband's pants for him when she saw that his own were badly outgrown. He went to work before and after school in 1869 at age eleven. Luckily for newspaper history, Adolph's first job was to be a carrier boy on the *Knoxville Chronicle*, then published by Capt. William Rule. As Ochs later wrote: "I had to appear at the office at five o'clock in the morning. The paper came from the press unfolded and the carrier boys had to fold the papers by hand. There were fifty papers to be delivered on my route and I had to walk nearly four miles to deliver them—then home to breakfast and thence to school. For this task I received twenty-five cents a day."

Adolph worked at the *Chronicle* for six years, becoming an office boy, a printer's devil, and finally a journeyman. At fourteen (presumably after his brief stint as an usher for Staub) he quit school to take a full-time job running errands and sweeping up in the newspaper offices. According to a story he liked to tell later, Adolph was free to leave at midnight but felt nervous about walking home alone in the dark past the old Presbyterian graveyard on State Street. Instead, he hung out at the office until one of the printers went off shift and could walk along with him. Meanwhile, in order to kill time, he practiced setting type, which was still done by hand. By the age of seventeen he had become a competent printer able to command a man's pay. To the end of his life, he was able to stand over a page of type and tell at a glance if it contained any errors. He always kept a great fondness for his first boss, Captain Rule, and later donated ten shares of *New York Times* stock to establish an annual William Rule/*New York Times* medal for the Knoxville high school student with the best grades. (Jack Neely, who discovered a record of this scholarship, couldn't find out what became of it.)

At age nineteen, Adolph teamed up with some Knoxville newspaper cronies to found a Chattanooga daily called the *Dispatch*, which failed within months. According to legend, he wanted to return home to Knoxville, but he didn't have enough money for a ticket and was ashamed to ask his family. So he stayed put, eventually finding success at age twenty, when he purchased the *Chattanooga Times*. Eighteen years later Adolph Ochs would buy the *New York Times* and turn that struggling daily into the nation's most prestigious newspaper. At the time, his mother objected strongly to the plan, even consulting relatives about whether her son could be restrained from this rash act on the grounds of mental disturbance. The local relatives apparently discouraged her from taking action, but were no more impressed with Adolph's plan.

One such relative was Jacob Blaufeld, whose mother was a relative of Julius Ochs. Blaufeld was a peddler when he first came to Knoxville in 1876 but soon thereafter started a successful cigar store on Gay Street. Under the management of Jacob, then his son, and finally another owner, who kept the same name, Blaufeld's was a fixture on the downtown scene for nearly a century. Selling tobacco products and light lunches of wurst and beans, the store was a meeting place for Jewish merchants and local politicians. Blaufeld's grandson Maurice

("Moose") Schwarzenberg, who still lives in Knoxville, recalls the family story that Jacob actually courted his cousin Adolph's sister for a while. The two men were friends, and when Jacob married Stella Nathan, Adolph sent some beautiful silverware that the Schwarzenberg family still owns. ("Of course, we can't ever use it, 'cause it has to stay in a vault all the time," he jokes.) When Adolph moved North, he asked his more affluent cousin to invest in the newspaper. Blaufeld declined on grounds the venture was much too risky and forever missed the chance to own a big piece of the *New York Times*. Apparently, there were no hard feelings and the two men remained close. When Adolph chose his newspaper's new slogan, "All the News That's Fit to Print," Jacob responded with a new slogan for his tobacco store: "All the Seegars Fit to Smoke." Unfortunately, Blaufeld chose to put his resources into the local Citizen Bank, of which he was a major stockholder. The family lost a fortune when the bank failed at the start of the Depression, and they were forced to close their store. Jacob's son Walter managed to open a smaller version in another downtown location, which survived for many decades as a place to buy cigars, newspapers, and standup lunches of beans with mettwurst and a dash of chili on top. I'm told it was also the best place in town to scalp University of Tennessee football tickets.

These were hardscrabble years in Knoxville, when fortunes could be easily made and quickly lost. The 1876 Knoxville city directory reported proudly that local population had "more than doubled" since the end of the war. The Jewish community was officially organized, but its small membership of German merchants had little time to spare for more than the barest observance. The monthly minyan moved around to various households until it settled in the basement of Jacob Spiro's Cider and Vinegar Works at 713 Gay Street, where the little congregation sat on vinegar barrels during services. The various Spiro brothers, all of whom had food businesses, were at the core of the little community. However, the only one I could find in the 1869 Helms City Directory was A. M. Spiro & Company on Gay Street, a confectionery whose cakes and candies are advertised under the stirring motto "as cheap as any other establishment in the city."

From early accounts it seems that Herman Spiro, who worked in the business, was particularly lauded for donating such baked goodies to the Sunday school and holiday gatherings.

The archives of Temple Beth El contain a written account of one such service in which "less than two minyans in number" gathered in a hall owned by "Messr. Spiro and Bros." Julius Ochs, who served as lay rabbi, was praised for his fine style in leading the service as well as for his sermons, which were two in English and two in German. It goes on to report that the service had "deep solemnity" and was "comparable with those in larger cities within the walls of their gorgeous temples." Music was performed by a trained choir from the local German *Turnverein*, accompanied by an organ. A year later, the congregation formally adopted the name Temple Beth El and voted to affiliate with the new Reform movement, which had originated in Germany and was now becoming especially popular in the Southern United States. About this time, Adolph married Iphigenia Miriam Wise, whose father, Isaac Mayer Wise, was generally considered to be the founder of Reform Judaism in America. Julius Ochs continued to serve as "minister" until later that year, when Adolph convinced the family to join him in Chattanooga. In a resignation letter to Temple president Emanuel Samuel, Julius confided that "nothing but dire

Jacob Spiro's Cider and Vinegar Works at 713 Gay Street was the site of early Jewish prayer services in Knoxville. Participants reportedly sat on vinegar barrels in the basement. Courtesy of Knoxville Jewish Federation.

necessity would have ever induced me to leave Knoxville—if God in his goodness and kindness should ever place me in a condition of independence again, Knoxville would be my choice." He never returned, but when Temple Beth El purchased its first building three decades later, wealthy publishing tycoon Adolph Ochs paid for its holy ark in memory of his parents.

Ten years after Adolph Ochs left, a man who would someday be his close friend moved to Knoxville. This German immigrant would also become wealthy and set an even stronger imprint on the Knoxville Jewish community. He settled here quite by accident. Max Arnstein immigrated to New York as a teenager, where he worked briefly in his uncle's clothing business. Later he was befriended by the family of wealthy financier Bernard Baruch and lived on the family's estate in Camden, South Carolina. As a young man, Arnstein was operating a store in Anderson, South Carolina, when Baruch's uncle Herman walked in and said, "Max, I came to have you join me in opening a new store in Birmingham, Alabama, which is on a big boom." After traveling to New York to load up a supply of goods, the pair were stranded for a week by the blizzard of 1888. By the time they made it as far as Knoxville, they had to rest for a while. Baruch looked around and said, "Max, this looks like a good town and there's a lot of stores to rent." They found a vacancy on Gay Street for one hundred dollars a month and proceeded to open, despite local predictions they would fail quickly. The venture did well from the start, and Arnstein bought his mentor Baruch's shares when the older man retired four years later. By 1905 he was wealthy enough to build Knoxville's first seven-story "skyscraper" on the corner of Union and Prince Street (later called Market). M. B. Arnstein & Company became a bastion of local elegance for the next two decades. It was the first modern department store in town, the kind of place where affluent women ordered custom-made gowns and shopped for Parisian lingerie. The graceful red-brick architecture of the building held up well over the decades. In the 1980s I had a marvelous fourth-floor window office in the Arnstein Building while working as an editor for 13-30 Corporation (which later became Whittle Communications). Today, the building still has numerous occupants, including *MetroPulse*. A giant photo mural in the downstairs lobby shows the store in its glory days, when electric streetcars brought fashionable

Knoxville to its front door. After Max Arnstein married the cultivated Lala Block of Galveston, Texas, the two became leaders in social philanthropy. Mrs. Arnstein once served on the Knox County Court, and the couple later made large donations to the University of Tennessee and the county library system. The childless couple lavished their greatest attention on the Jewish community, helping underwrite its first permanent home.

The young congregation was growing. Temple minutes from 1877 refer to a Sunday school, though it seems to have operated sporadically in the first years. A clipping from the gossip column of the *Knoxville Journal* dated June 20, 1886, reports, "A few months since the Jewish citizens of Knoxville organized a Sunday school. At first the school had but few members, but now it is a strong body of earnest workers. The school has attained such proportions that it had to seek new quarters, and is now held every Sunday morning from 9 to 10:30 o'clock in the K. of H. [Knights of Honour] hall." (Just below this item is a report that "Oscar Wilde talks of coming back and says he won't mind the ocean trip so long as he can get plenty of Dr. Bull's Cough Syrup to kill off colds.") In a short history of Temple Beth El written for its eightieth anniversary, Anne Marcovitch wrote: "Soon after the school was organized, Herman Spiro offered it a room in his modest home. . . . Many a holiday celebration was turned into a gala affair by the sweets, tidbits and other gifts brought in by the enthusiastic Mr. Spiro. For many years the religious school held forth in Mr. Spiro's home. Then it started on its wandering course, moving from pillar to post, usually following the congregation as they moved from one hall to another."

On High Holidays, when attendance reached its annual peak, services were held at the Masonic Temple, the Lyceum Building, or various other rented halls. Several times, at the invitation of progressive pastor Dr. James Park, High Holiday services were conducted at the First Presbyterian Church. (However, the records show that not all church elders were happy about lending their premises to Jews. To avoid offense, it was arranged that the Jewish congregation should enter by the back door.)

By early 1888 a committee had raised sufficient funds to hire a student rabbi from Cincinnati's Hebrew Union College to officiate at

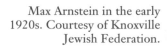

Max Arnstein in the early
1920s. Courtesy of Knoxville
Jewish Federation.

Arnstein's Department Store
at the corner of Prince (now Union)
and Market Streets was Knoxville's
first seven-story "skyscraper" and
perhaps the most elegant
establishment in town. Courtesy of
Knoxville Jewish Federation.

High Holiday Services. Leo Franklin became the first of a series of student rabbis hired on an irregular basis over the next thirty-four years. Some of these students became well-known rabbis in later years. Harold Winston's history in the 1964 Temple Beth El Centennial Book lists the student rabbis as follows:

Leo Franklin	1888, 1890
David Marx	1891
George Zepin	1898
Jacob Kaplan	1899, 1900
Julian Morgenstern	
(later president of UAHC)	1901
Jacob D. Schwarrz	1903
J. Blau	1905
Oscar Berman	1907, 1908
Jacob Tarshish	1911
James G. Heller	1913
Gary August	1915, 1916, 1917, 1918
Samuel J. Harris	1919
Henry J. Berkowitz	1920
Ferdinand Isserman	1921
Sol Landman	1922

Also in 1888 the Temple membership was enlarged with men who would become important community leaders and, in several cases, father subsequent generations of leaders: Max B. Arnstein, Solomon David, David Rosenthal, Abe David, Max Lobenstein, Henry Bloom, Henry Goodfriend, Henry Friedman, Jacob Reich, Simon Sunshine, Simon Deitch, Joe Schier, and L. Schwartz. Bolstered by this support, the congregation began to seek a permanent house of worship. In the time-honored tradition of such things, a committee was appointed to seek pledges and found guarded success when several individuals committed to the substantial sum of one hundred dollars each. Yet the right building at the right price was never found during the next two years of searching, and quite a few members resigned.

The turn of the century was apparently a low point in the Temple's fortunes. Membership declined markedly in the early 1890s as Knoxville Jewish families switched to the new Heska Amuna Orthodox congregation. In any case, Temple Beth El voted to reorganize under a new state charter for Knoxville Hebrew Congregation Beth El issued on January 4, 1893. It lost no time in obtaining a new cemetery according to records, which relate: "Finding the cemetery small and very unsuitable in February 1893, the Congregation . . . purchased five acres near the present terminus of the Middlebrook car line." From the outset, both congregations used this new cemetery. One of the most active Temple organizations at that time was the Jewish Study Circle, a group of ten young ladies who met twice each month for the purpose of studying Jewish topics. This group, first organized by student rabbi George Zepin in 1898, became active as teachers and substitutes in the new Sunday school. By 1903 Chattanooga Rabbi Leo Mannheimer came to Knoxville twice a month for services, Sunday school and an adult Bible class. The study circle's minutes for October 10 record that "The syllabus for the course 'History of the Jews from Mishna to Mendelssohn' (prepared by Mr. Mannheimer) were received."

The chance to finally purchase a Temple building came in 1914, largely through the efforts of increasingly wealthy Max Arnstein. He later described the purchase in this way: "In my former town, where not a dozen Jews were living, it was my habit to go to Church on Sunday morning. In Knoxville, I was attracted occasionally to the services held by Dr. Frazee. He was a Congregational Minister, a Bostonian, with all the traditional learning and culture. . . . One day towards the end of the 1890s, Dr. Frazee surprised me with a visit and told me this story. 'You have been at my church and noticed the small attendance. My Board in Boston deems it futile to carry on longer. We have a valuable and costly church property but must sell it. Would the Jewish people, not having a temple, be interested in buying?'" Given Beth El's membership troubles, it took about fifteen years to raise the necessary pledges from members and several Christian friends. With Arnstein as the largest contributor, the Plymouth Congregational Church on Vine Avenue and Broadway was purchased for five thousand dollars. Rabbi George Zepin came back to preside over this event, but Temple Beth El would make do with student rabbis until it was able to hire its first permanent rabbi, Jerome Mark, in 1922. (Dr. Frazee, as luck would have it, was a next-door neighbor of Simon Levy—David Levy's ancestor—who was one of Knoxville's most successful saloonkeepers.)

In 1929, the Arnsteins decided to sell off their store's inventory and retire to New York City. In practice this meant that Arnstein liquidated his assets on the eve of the Great Depression, when the relatively few men who held cash reserves in a cash-starved economy remained wealthy. This piece of good fortune would become a watershed event in the life of the Knoxville Jewish community, for Arnstein's 1929 gift of a building adjoining the Temple (along with many later gifts of cash and real estate) would make the Knoxville Jewish Community Center possible.

The founding of Heska Amuna Orthodox congregation signals that another group of Jews had begun to arrive in Knoxville just as young Max Arnstein and his fellow German-Jewish merchants were beginning to achieve success in business. This third and largest wave of Jews came from the ghettos of Eastern Europe. "In 1880 there were perhaps two hundred fifty thousand Jews in the United States, a few of them Jews who had come during the colonial period and most of the rest German Jews and their descendents. Fewer than 50,000 were from Eastern Europe," notes Roger Daniels in *Coming to America: A History of Immigration and Ethnicity in American Life*. "When, in 1924, Congress cut immigration from Europe down to almost nothing, there were perhaps four million Jews in the United States, more than three million of them Eastern Europeans and their children and grandchildren."

These immigrants fled the deadly peasant riots called pogroms, the increasing persecutions of Tsarist government, and the harsh fate of conscription into the Russian army. Immigrant neighborhoods such as the Lower East Side of New York became so overcrowded that many left in search of a better living. Fortunately, the postwar southern economy was starting to pick up steam just as this flood of East European Jewish immigration accelerated in the late 1880s. In nearly every rural corner of the South, Jewish peddlers arrived to supply the farmers who were just beginning to have spare cash again. "Think of the first meeting of the peddler and the Southerner," suggests Eli Evans, who invokes this dramatic image in *The Provincials*, his history-cum-memoir of Jewish life in the American South. "The Jew, back-bent and weary, trudging the dusty back roads, stumbling past the yelping hound dogs and the chickens, to be met at the porch of a patched-up shack by the blue-eyed Aryan with a rifle across his chest and his wife behind him with the children peering around her skirt. The Jew, hesitating momentarily and then motioning to his pack and stammering, 'It goot—you buy?'—bowing and obsequious, only to serve and sell. What must these two men have thought of each other?" Yet the intersection of these two cultures—one large, one tiny by comparison—would have a lasting impact on towns across the South.

The late Jake Corkland, born in Knoxville in 1901, recalled in a written essay that his own father, Gerson, and a dozen other founders of Heska Amuna Synagogue arrived with the help of a Jewish relief organization which was trying to help new immigrants move

Interior of Gerson Corkland's store at Central and Willow Streets in the Old City. His son Jake is pictured inside. Courtesy of Knoxville Jewish Federation.

away from overcrowded Eastern cities. His memoir credits this help to the Hebrew Immigrant Aid Society (HIAS) but it was more likely a function of the Industrial Removal Office, set up in 1901 by the Baron de Hirsch Fund to relieve the density of Jewish population on the Atlantic seaboard. The IRO operated for about two decades, dispatching immigrants to settlements as far away as Portland, as well as southern communities with only a handful of Jewish residents. According to historian Lee Shai Weissbach, merchants in dozens of small southern towns acted as agents for the IRO, helping immigrants get settled and reporting back on their progress.

Of course, this charitable endeavor was only one force moving Jews to the South. Big wholesale businesses such as the Peddler Supply Company and Jacob Epstein's Baltimore Bargain House became de facto resettlement agencies, dispensing information on how and where to get started. Under the most popular scheme, a pack full of merchandise would be furnished on credit. The new-minted businessman would head south, hoping to turn over his merchandise, buy more, prosper, and eventually find a place to settle. If all went well, the peddler became a merchant with a small store. He sent for his wife and children and brought over his brothers and his cousins. The Bargain House not only extended credit to start peddlers in business but also gave established peddlers a free train ticket back to Baltimore when it was time to restock. In this way, novice peddlers, often lacking in English and any knowledge of the South, listened to the returning veterans for advice on the best routes, the danger spots, and the towns in which a "greener" might get some friendly help from other Jews.

Cattle broker Sam Lavine arrived in East Tennessee via the famous Baltimore Bargain House. "He came to Knoxville in the late 1880s, during Cleveland's administration," explained his son-in-law Max Weinstein in a taped interview conducted a hundred years later by Barbara Bernstein:

> The head of the Baltimore Bargain House was well-acquainted with M. B. Arnstein. He told Sam, "You go to Knoxville, it's a good town, they'll get you started peddling so you can learn the language." M. B. Arnstein fixed him up with a pack and a horse-and-wagon. So he

got it loaded up with his pins and needles and threads and started down Gay Street, over the bridge. Where to go, he don't know. As he got on the bridge he let the reins loose. One road went to [what is now] Alcoa, one to the Old Sevierville Road. He said to himself, "Whichever way the horse goes, I'll go." What difference did it make—he didn't know where he was going anyhow. The horse turned left and he went to Sevierville. Sam learned to talk pretty good and people down there started to like him. I remember he told me, "I sold curtain goods to women who didn't even have a window." One of his new friends urged him to get into cattle, so he bought a steer or two and sold it at a nice profit. After that he was in the cattle business. He bought more livestock than anybody in Sevier County.

For the record, Max's son Sanford, whom his wife, Myra Corkland Weinstein, claims was by far the better historian, heard his grandfather tell the story a little differently. By Sanford's account, Sam actually let his mule—not a horse—make the key decision at the junction between the Sevierville and Knoxville roads from the north, which was why he didn't initially settle near the rest of the Jewish community.

At any rate, Sevier County in this era was an isolated, dirt-poor, often lawless region that was always distrustful of strangers. Yet Sam Lavine made a lot of friends. It was said that if he bought some widow's cattle and resold it for more profit than he expected, he'd return the extra money to the widow. One of the stranger episodes in local Jewish history involved Sam's friendship with various members of the White Caps, a local white vigilante group. Apparently, one of the White Caps was going to be hanged for murder after a famous battle with the Blue Bills—a rival citizen's militia. Sam loaded the man's soon-to-be widow and seven children into a wagon and drove them all the way to Nashville to plead for clemency from the governor. The plea was unsuccessful, but people in the county remembered Sam gratefully. Eventually, Sam brought his own family over and moved the cattle business to Knoxville, where he was a founding member of Heska Amuna Congregation in 1890. After his wife passed away, he lived for

Delivery truck for M. Licht's Bottling Works, circa World War I. The company, which now makes condiments, is still operated in Knoxville by Richard Licht. Courtesy of Richard Licht.

some time with his daughter Gertrude Weinstein and her husband, Max, who came to Knoxville in the 1920s to manage a shoe store. Recalls Weinstein, "Sam used to smoke cigars and drink liquor like nobody's business—though I never saw him drunk—and he still died at 97."

The Lavine, Weinstein, and Corkland families were linked up a generation ago when Jake's daughter Myra married Max's son Sanford. It was another steaming day in early fall—the week of Sukkot, the harvest festival—when Myra Corkland Weinstein drove me downtown in the spic-and-span coupe she uses for real estate clients. Myra began her real estate career in the 1960s, when urban renewal was obliterating the downtown Vine Avenue neighborhood, where so many Jewish homes and businesses once stood. One of her first jobs was to relocate the last, mostly elderly residents who still lived and owned dwindling businesses in this area. That fall day, Myra and I parked at the Hyatt Regency Hotel over by the Coliseum, and took the elevator up to the top floor. It was a clear day, so we could peer out a side window to the mountain pass where her Lithuanian immigrant grandfather first entered Tennessee. "Gerson decided to look for a town that offered three things: A doctor, a Jewish community, and a school for the children," says Myra. "Knoxville had all that."

Later, she drove me down to the corner of Jackson and Central Avenues in the Old City. At the turn of the century, it was a rowdy part of town full of beer halls and cheap stores. Myra imagines her grandfather sitting on this corner, wearing fingerless gloves on a cold winter day as he sold hot roasted potatoes to passersby. According to family legend, he was engaged in this business one day when an elegant lady in a carriage noticed how hard he was working. The lady was Emily Burr, niece of the famous politician-duelist Aaron Burr. She convinced her family (including George Burr, who operated a lumber business) to help Gerson build a small mercantile store at the corner of Central and Willow Streets. Years later, Jake Corkland recalled childhood Sunday outings when the entire Corkland family would drive out to lay flowers at the north Knoxville cemetery, where Emily Burr was buried. The building that housed their Old City grocery and mercantile shop still exists, occupied today by a funky costume rental store called Big Don's. The Corkland family originally occupied apartments in the back during the first years, separated from the store by a sliding glass door. One night when Gerson was minding shop, a party of Spanish American War soldiers walked in. One was very drunk. When the store didn't have what this soldier wanted, he stuck his bayonet on the end of his rifle and prepared to stab Gerson. Seeing all this through the glass door, Gerson's wife, Janet, ran out with her cast-iron frying pan and knocked the soldier out cold. Myra still has that frying pan. "And I still cook with it," she adds.

In 1880 so many Jewish peddlers were floating through Knoxville that the new Ladies Hebrew Benevolent Auxiliary—grown weary of providing personal hospitality—began to collect funds to house and feed transients at local boardinghouses. A decade later, several dozen of these new arrivals had established small businesses around Vine Street, begun to bring over their families, and established their own synagogue. A city directory for 1900 shows an increasing number of Eastern Europeans among the fifty-some identifiably Jewish families

Isaac Coplan's grocery on University Avenue in Knoxville, late 1880s. His grandchildren Gilbert Levison and Natalie Levison Robinson still live in town. Courtesy of Knoxville Jewish Federation.

living in Knoxville. The new immigrants generally spoke Yiddish, the Hebrew-German patois of the Eastern European ghettos. They were steeped in the traditional religious observances and dietary laws that the Reform movement Temple Beth El had begun to cast off. The entire East Tennessee Jewish community numbered only a few hundred souls, but the German *Juden* and the Eastern European *Yidden* would soon go their separate ways. ∞

Three

TempleJews
and Synagogue Jews

'm looking at a 1918 portrait of Temple Beth El's first confirmation class, graduated four years after the move into a new building on Vine Street. The photograph shows four handsome teenagers posed in a glowing moment of bourgeois elegance at the end of World War I. Morton Deitch looks stiff but proud in his dark suit and high, starched collar; Clara Katz, Blanche Konigsberg, and Flora Bart cluster gracefully on either side in white lace dresses and enormous hair bows, each one clasping a large arrangement of beribboned flowers.

These are the children of Knoxville's increasingly prosperous German Jews. They represent perhaps one-tenth of 1 percent of Knoxville's 97,000 citizens, but most of these German-Jewish families are now firmly established in local business circles. The younger generation speaks English with no accent but the high twang of East Tennessee. They are earnestly all-American, energetically involved in the cultural and civic life of their community. Clara Katz, a talented violinist, will soon take a chair in Knoxville's new symphony orchestra. (She also plays the haunting melody of the Kol Nidre prayer in front of the ark at the Temple every Yom Kippur.) At the moment, her mother is trying to get her to step out socially with classmate Morton Deitch, but Clara's eyes are fixed elsewhere. At any rate, Morton won't be long for this town; he'll graduate from Yale with top honors and go on to become a partner in one of New York City's most prominent law firms.

Temple Beth El's first confirmation class, 1918. *Left to right, back row:* Morton Deitch, Flora Brody, and student rabbi Gary August. *Front row, left to right:* Blanche Konigsberg and Clara Katz. Courtesy of Barbara Winick Bernstein.

Teachers and students pose at Temple Beth El's annual Sunday school picnic at Chilhowee Park, circa 1917. Courtesy of Dr. Harold Winston.

The Lippner family, proprietors of a butcher's stall in the old Market House, were typical of settled, middle-class German Jewry before World War I. Their affluence and determination to fit smoothly into Gentile society differed markedly from the more recently arrived Eastern European *Yidden*, who tended to observe more traditional Jewish practice. Courtesy of Knoxville Jewish Federation.

By no means does that imply that Knoxville lacks genteel diversion in 1918. Fannie, Katie, and Harry Lippner, whose father and uncle share a butcher's stall in the Market House, have formed a little orchestra that plays for dinner hour at the Old Imperial Hotel on Gay Street. Fannie (who would later be Fannie Stein) goes down to play the chimes at Kuhlman's Drug Store every day at noon. The children spend summers in the foothills at the elegant Neubert Springs Hotel. In the hotel's dance pavilion, they learn the two-step and the waltz. A few summers before, they traveled out to the hotel in a horse-drawn hack, but Harry came to bring them home in his first Ford, which "seemed to fly" as it covered the ten-mile trip in thirty minutes.

Ben Allen, a Jewish policeman, directs traffic from a box on Gay Street. Jacob Reich's grocery store on Vine Street has become a gathering place for local farmers, who can stable their horses at Vine Street and Central in order to settle in for a day's shopping and conversation. Miriam Reich, aged five, spends Saturdays behind the cigar counter, watching her mother expertly cut and roll tobacco. Not long before this, Jacob Reich, Morris Bart, and their friend David Rosenthal (whose drugstore is another favorite hangout for Knoxvillians) traveled to Chattanooga to take exams that would admit them as thirty-second-degree Scottish Rite Masons. A photo of these men among the Scottish Rite graduation class of 1908 is proudly displayed in the Reich home. Morris Bart, a Knoxville clothing merchant since the 1890s, is active in the local chamber of commerce, while the prominent Mrs. Rose Deitch of the Temple eventually will become state president of the PTA.

Every spring, Temple Beth El's young children look forward to the annual Sunday school picnic. Everyone gathers at the main trolley depot on Gay Street for a trip to the wide-open fields of Chilhowee Park. Dressed in their fine white sailor suits and boaters, clutching little bags of popcorn, the children look and act like any other middle-class Sunday school group in the city. Many Temple Beth El members no longer keep the Jewish dietary laws, which require abstention from pork and shellfish as well as the strict separation of meat items from dairy items. Their Reform Sabbath services are held on Sunday, using very little Hebrew, while their men have abandoned the skullcaps, prayer shawls, and phylacteries that once set all Jewish worshippers so vividly apart from the Christian neighbors. No Hebrew instruction is given to the children in the Temple Sunday school in 1918, and it will be five more years before the congregation celebrates a bar mitzvah. (It would try this experiment briefly, only to abandon it again for nearly two decades, until the bar mitzvah of Bob Freeman in 1956.)

As the confirmation class poses for its photo, another group of Jewish schoolchildren is gathered at the opposite end of Vine Street in the basement of Mrs. Pearl Collins's family home. The only girl present is ten-year-old Sarah Green, since most of the Orthodox families in Heska Amuna Congregation don't give their daughters the same

Heska Amuna Synagogue Religious School, early 1900s. Courtesy of Knoxville Jewish Federation.

rigorous Hebrew education drilled into their sons. It's the traditional way. Luckily, Sarah's parents, who run a small grocery on Broadway, are tolerant of her interest in Hebrew learning. Her Russian immigrant father, Joseph Green, is a Talmud scholar in his own right, so the eight Green children absorb a lot of Jewish learning at home. Within a year or two, Sarah will be proficient enough to help tutor the younger boys for bar mitzvah, the coming-of-age ritual in which a thirteen-year-old male is called to the Torah to read Hebrew blessings and some part of that week's portion of holy Scripture. She herself will never approach the *bima* (altar), where the scrolls are stored, and never handle a Sefer Torah.

The method of instruction at the little *cheder,* or Hebrew school, is quite simple. The children cluster around a long wooden table with chairs on either side. The immigrant *melamed,* or Hebrew teacher, lives in a curtained-off area in one corner of the basement, just large enough to hold his bed, a table, and a small gas ring for cooking. While the children read Hebrew prayers aloud in noisy unison, the *melamed* retires behind his curtain to boil himself a glass of tea. Whenever the voices began to waver, his Yiddish roar is heard from behind the curtain: *"Nochamol!"* ("Do it again!"). If the boys don't pay attention, the melamed's long stick will come down on their knuckles. He has a difficult time maintaining the discipline of the Eastern European *shtetl*, or Jewish settlement, for the Knoxville children love to play tricks on the bushy-bearded teacher. Their parents, too, have begun to depart from some of the Old World customs. Most married women no longer cover their hair with kerchiefs or the traditional wigs, called *sheytls*. The men go to pray early in the morning on Shabbat, then open their stores, because Saturday is Knoxville's biggest shopping day. They try to get along with the Gentiles. "We were a little afraid to flaunt the fact that we were Jewish, that we didn't eat *chazer* [pig]," remembers Sarah many decades later. "If I was out with the other schoolgirls, I would just say I wasn't hungry."

In the winter of 1999, Sarah Green Robinson, age ninety-one, still cuts a stylish figure in the middle pews of Heska Amuna Synagogue on Shabbat morning. My eleven-year-old daughter loves to sit with Mrs. Robinson, who always seems to have a Tootsie Roll in her purse for

The Temperance Avenue Synagogue of Heska Amuna Congregation, used 1893–1920. Courtesy of Barbara Winick Bernstein.

Temple Beth El's building on Broadway and Vine Street, used 1914–57. Courtesy of Knoxville Jewish Federation.

Anna, plus an extra sweet for Anna's younger brother, David. Sabbath morning services at our synagogue are quite lengthy but conducted with informality that often startles visitors less familiar with traditional Jewish rites. Prayer goes on for nearly three hours, but against the backdrop of Hebrew chant there are many opportunities to greet one's friends or hold whispered conversations. During one such exchange, Sarah and Anna compared birthdays and were pleased to discover they were both born and raised in the Knoxville Jewish community—exactly eight days less than eighty years apart.

On a weekday morning, I went to visit Mrs. Robinson at her handsome apartment in Sequoyah Hills, located a few blocks from the home of her daughter Joyce Robinson Diftler, a local psychotherapist. The other children and grandchildren have scattered, but Mrs. Robinson keeps up with them by e-mail on her computer. Family is everything, she tells me vigorously. Her own parents had eight children, and she was married at age eighteen to one of the five Robinson brothers. "Growing up, I didn't need many friends," she says. "I had family, and that was enough."

After Sarah's father, Joseph, left his small town in Russia, he settled in London. Down the street from where he boarded was a man named Joe Green, who sold bananas from a cart. So when a government clerk asked for his name, Sarah's father identified himself as "Joe Green." Eventually he made his way to Knoxville because a brother-in-law had settled here. At first Joe peddled ice cream at a penny a cone, but when he managed to open a small store, he sent for Sarah's mother and the oldest children. The Greens' store sold overalls and dry goods to railroad employees, but Sarah remembers that her father always carried bananas out front. Sometimes the beat policeman would walk by, grab a banana from the bunch, and keep walking. *"Chazer,"* Joe would growl under his breath. Sarah can remember that the Old City Race Riot of 1919, which flared after the murder of a white woman led to the arrest of a black man. Many Jewish businesses on Vine Street were shut down for several days as army troops were sent in to quell the disturbance. Machine guns were posted on the roof of one Jewish building as tensions flared between white rioters and black residents who lived in tenements east of the Old City. Sarah remembers creeping to the front window of the family store to watch armed soldiers running down the street. Her father shouted at her "Get away from there! Get down!" For a man who remembered violent peasant riots against the Jews of Russia, the event must have been terrifying.

Heska Amuna Synagogue had been organized nearly two decades before in 1890. East Europeans formed the backbone of the new Orthodox *shul* (the Yiddish word for synagogue). This was part of a common pattern in southern communities, according to historian Lee Shai Weissbach. He comments in a recent article for *American*

Jewish History that "the newly arrived East Europeans frequently organized congregations that functioned alongside pre-existing assemblies, for the immigrants were uncomfortable in these older congregations, which had almost invariably adopted Reform practice by the end of the nineteenth century." Heska Amuna actually received early support from several established German families, but most of them (or their descendants) switched back to membership in Temple Beth El by the 1920s. A memoir written by Barbara Bernstein's aunt, Ida Winick Siegel, some decades later listed only fifteen member families at Temple Beth El in 1900, compared with forty-five member families at Heska Amuna. Since Mrs. Siegel (who, by all accounts, had a crackerjack memory for such details) listed the names of those who belonged to each institution that year, it becomes easy to see that a number of Synagogue families or their descendants later rejoined the Temple.

Somewhat to the amusement of its rabbis down through the years, the name "Heska Amuna" is actually a spelling mistake. Apparently, the *shul's* immigrant founders weren't sure how to render the Hebrew words *Chaskei Emunah*, or "Strongholders of the Faith," into English letters. Once written into a state charter, however, Heska Amuna became the official version, though other spellings floated around for a while. In any case, the new group quickly found a small house at Vine and Temperance Streets to use as a synagogue, and in 1895 they hired immigrant Rabbi Isaac Winick as their rabbi. True to the usual priorities, Heska Amuna first organized a school for children, then worked on creating a sanctuary for worship in the Temperance Avenue building. When the sanctuary was completed in 1902, the elders of the community put on skullcaps and *tallisim* (prayer shawls), then paraded down Gay Street with the scrolls of the Torah in their arms. Their willingness to do this indicates a surprising degree of comfort with displaying their most sacred ritual objects in front of the downtown Gentile merchants. One can scarcely imagine it happening even in our own ecumenical time. Of course, since Knoxville's population of more than thirty-two thousand citizens contained fewer than sixty Jewish families in 1902, the action may not have made a big splash. Turn-of-the-century Knoxville contained a large number of immigrant ethnic groups, most of whose members lived, worked, and socialized downtown. Parades

Rabbi Isaac Winick's sons and their friends played baseball in the backyard of Heska Amuna's Temperance Avenue Synagogue, where the rabbi's family lived. Courtesy of Barbara Winick Bernstein.

were extremely common, being among the many impromptu entertainments afforded by the lively city streets.

Sarah Robinson recalls that the old sanctuary at Temperance and Vine Avenue included a snuffbox up on the *bima*, or altar, so that after being called to the Torah, each man might take a *"smeckl tabac."* (This occurred even on the Sabbath and Yom Kippur, Sarah assured me.) Rabbi Winick and his family lived in the same building, and their quarters contained the *mikveh*, or ritual bath in which married women immersed themselves after their monthly periods. This traditional purification ritual (also used by men at other intervals) goes back to antiquity, but modesty has usually tended to keep Jewish women from discussing the matter very much. Sarah has memories of eating sweets in the parlor while her mother went to the back room for what seemed to be a very mysterious monthly business—not fully revealed until just before her own wedding.

Meanwhile, in the front yard, Rabbi Winick's three sons played baseball with their friends. Out in the backyard, chickens were slaughtered according to strict *kashrut*, the Jewish dietary laws. Over the years, some changes were made. Other kosher butchers operated in

The redoubtable Mrs. Fanny Beiler *(back row, wearing a hat)* poses with her Temple Beth El Sunday school class around 1918. Courtesy of Dr. Harold Winston.

downtown Knoxville. A regular Sunday school for boys and girls began meeting in the shul, though separate Hebrew training for the boys was continued. Post–bar mitzvah training was not stressed for some time; it was 1933 before Heska Amuna's first confirmation class was graduated.

Oddly, the standard Orthodox custom of separating men and women during prayer was abandoned almost immediately in the early years of the century. Some people credit the many strong, involved women leaders in the community for this decision, though few surviving documents record the names of those women. The legacy of these early Jewish women is more established at the Temple, where sisters Fanny Liebman Beiler and Rose Liebman Deitch held sway over the Sunday school and Sisterhood for decades. Fanny ran the Sunday school and Rose headed the Sisterhood. Their husbands (both of whom were downtown businessmen) served repeatedly as presidents of the Temple and Men's Club but seemed to have been closely coached in these functions by their redoubtable wives. Industrious and respectable in the extreme, the few surviving photos of these sisters show them perennially hatted, gloved, and tightly corseted, the sort of women who worried mightily how to make Judaism fit in smoothly with the ethics and aesthetics of the city's other religious denominations. One story relates how Fanny Beiler disapproved strongly of a certain Temple woman who had an affair with a married member. The man in question later divorced his wife, married his lover, and had several children. Mrs. Beiler supposedly refused to enroll these children in the Temple Sunday school on the grounds that they were fruit of a poisoned tree. What is unquestionably true is that Mrs. Beiler was known to work tirelessly for Temple Beth El. By the time her tenure ended, the once-struggling Sunday school was firmly established as an institution in the city's Jewish communal life.

Knoxville was numbered among southern Jewish communities which showed early, vigorous support for Zionism. Ida Winick Siegel's memoir relates that an Ohavel Zion Society (forerunner of the Zionist District) was formed in Knoxville by 1900. Sam Lavine's daughter, Gert Weinstein, formed a Knoxville chapter of Hadassah in the late 1920s. This, too, was part of the pattern in smaller southern towns with a heavy proportion of Eastern European immigrants. "Perhaps the most visible of all American Zionist societies in the interwar period (as today) was the women's organization Hadassah, founded by Henrietta Szold in 1912 to raise funds for health care and other projects in Palestine and to promote Jewish education in the United States," notes Lee Shai Weissbach. "Thus, in the years before mid-century, the presence of a Hadassah chapter in a town was a very good indicator of Zionist activism at the local level. It is significant, therefore, that in the period before World War II Hadassah chapters sprang up not only in the principal cities of the South but also in many of the small towns to which Eastern European immigrants had moved."

My friend Mary Linda Schwarzbart lent me an intriguing stack of official minutes from the Knoxville Hadassah meetings of the late 1920s and early 1930s. Far more Heska Amuna women were listed as attendees, though Temple Beth El was represented by a few members (notably Mrs. Phillip Chazen and Miss S. R. Deitch, whose families remained firm Zionists into the next generation.) A "junior" Hadassah group was eventually started to serve the needs of young single women in Knoxville. By 1928, the combined junior and senior wings of the Knoxville chapter included forty female members—representing as much as half of the total Jewish households.

The presence of strong women aside, a definite cultural gulf yawned between Temple and Synagogue leadership during this period. Knoxville's Orthodox Jews seemed determined to stick with practices that held them apart from their Christian neighbors, while the Reform Jews were equally determined to minimize those differences. "Back then, we thought the Temple people were *goyim*," recalls Sarah Green Robinson dryly, using the Yiddish word for "non-Jew." "They ate *tref* [nonkosher food] and didn't cover their heads to pray on Shabbos." ("Of course, that's all changed now," she adds hastily. "I have plenty of friends at the Temple. Still . . ." Her voice trails off. I can complete the sentence for her, though. The two groups were separate camps then, and so they have always remained.)

Still another gulf between Temple and Synagogue was economic. The German merchant Jews had mostly arrived earlier, with more secular education, and by this time quite a few had flourishing businesses in the downtown area. Partly for this reason, members of Knoxville's Temple Beth El tended to be much more involved in the general community in the first two decades of this century. According to some reports, a few very affluent Temple families actually belonged to Knoxville's oh-so-exclusive Cherokee Country Club during this time. This was particularly significant, because after Knoxville voted to close its approximately one hundred saloons in 1907, the "dry" city became a place where much business and social intercourse was conducted at the private clubs, speakeasies, and homes where liquor was served. A membership in Cherokee was the ticket to Knoxville's highest society and most rarefied business dealings. By the Depression era, however, Cherokee would become notorious for its unspoken policy of refusing membership to Jews and African Americans.

Ironically, the more traditional immigrant *Yidden* of the Synagogue here and elsewhere often had less "foreign" last names than the more assimilated *Juden* at the Temple. The first wave of German

This elegant group is probably the Men's Club of Temple Beth El, at a formal dinner in the late 1920s. Courtesy of Knoxville Jewish Federation.

Jewish settlers tended to keep original surnames such as Blaufeld, Katz, Deitch, and Konigsburg. Wearing these names could sometimes make life uncomfortable during World War I, when anti-German sentiments rose. By contrast, many East European Jews took brand-new monikers around the time they arrived in America. This occurred in a variety of ways. Sometimes employers or government officials substituted Americanized names for ones they found too hard to spell. In many other cases, the first Jewish immigrant in a family was a young male who arrived on forged papers to escape army recruitment officials at Russian ports. Relatives who followed him adopted the same name on shipping manifests in order to ease their passage through Ellis Island. This process turned the two Dobrzhinski boys of Poland into Max and Nathan Burnett of Knoxville, while the six Rabinowitz brothers became Robinsons. According to family legend, the first immigrant in the Tobe family of Knoxville got his new name because he couldn't spell the old one on an official form. The attending clerk wrote in "to be announced," which the new immigrant obligingly abbreviated into his new surname.

The roster of the Synagogue shows dozens of names that could easily have been listed on the passenger rolls of the *Mayflower*—Collins, Green, Thorpe, Berry, Brown, Miller. Even some of those who arrived with their family names mostly intact later opted for a more Anglicized version. Moscowitz became Morrison and Fayonsky became Fay. (My own maiden name is Lowe, which actually comes from Gentile relatives on my father's side. Yet American Jewry contains so many Lowes whose family names were once Lowenstein or Loebenthal that I remember my mother being queried more than once by other Jews: "So—what was it before?")

Using the hindsight of a more tolerant age, it can be easy to forget why many Jews in that era were so eager to blend in. "The major impetus toward assimilation was the growth of public anti-Semitism," writes Malcolm Stern in *Turn to the South*, a collection of essays on southern Jewish history. In 1877 the family of prominent banker Joseph Seligman was denied admission to a fashionable resort in upstate New York. The resultant battle in the press only fanned the "America for Americans" fervor that had already begun to rise partly in response to waves of Jewish immigration from Eastern Europe. (It bears noting that according to *Our Crowd* author Stephen Birmingham, the Seligmans named one of their sons George Washington Seligman and another Alfred Lincoln Seligman out of fear that Abraham Lincoln Seligman would sound too Jewish!) "The 1870s inaugurated a change in the view of American Jewry held by the general populace," writes Dan A. Oren in *Joining the Club: A History of Jews and Yale*. "By the end of the decade, when Jews began to be publicly excluded from upper-class social circles, it became evident that the bounds of prejudice in American society were expanding."

For decades, the genteel brand of social anti-Semitism kept Jews out of exclusive clubs, led to restrictive covenants against Jews in many neighborhoods, and produced quota systems in universities and professions. Upscale Jews sought to counter this situation not only by attempting to fit in but also by educating the general public. "A prime function of the Southern rabbi became interpreting the Jew to the non-Jewish community," writes Stern. Reform temples in particular wanted rabbis who were clean-shaven, accent-free, and easily able to mingle with the local clergy. (Photos of rabbis at Heska Amuna and Temple Beth El before World War I show this contrast between the poles of Jewish society. Orthodox Rabbi Isaac Winick, bearded and prophetlike, sits stiffly in a chair wearing East European head covering and caftan; clean-shaven Reform student rabbi Gary August is fashionable in his Western suit, leaning nonchalantly against a Model-T Ford.)

As luck would have it, Knoxville played a role in shaping the efforts of Reform Jews to make their religious life more palatable to the Gentile world. Malcolm Stern relates that in 1910, the Jewish Chatauqua Society, which was organized in the late 1890s to train Jews in Judaism, received a request from the chancellor of the University of Tennessee at Knoxville for a speaker on the Bible. Julian Morgenstern, then a young college professor and later the much-acclaimed president of Hebrew Union College, was dispatched to give three lectures. Though fundamentalist preachers in Tennessee raised an almighty fuss against having a Jew indoctrinate their young people, Morgenstern's University of Tennessee lectures were so successful that the Jewish Chatauqua Society changed its entire program to center around instructing Christians about Judaism.

When Julian Morgenstern returned to Knoxville in the fall of 1901 to conduct High Holiday services at Temple Beth El, he became instrumental in helping revive the almost moribund Temple membership. Heska Amuna's new Orthodox congregation had pulled substantial numbers of Jewish families away from the struggling Temple, particularly after its first attempt to secure a building failed. A city directory of churches from 1900 reflects the relative positions of its two "Hebrew" congregations. Beth El, not yet having a settled home, is listed as "Meets first Sunday of each month" with the names of its current officers (F. Heart, president; L. David, vice president; S. Hyman, treasurer; S. Burger, secretary). Apparently, it still followed the classical Reform custom of shifting the Jewish Sabbath to Sunday, where it fit more smoothly with Gentile customs. "Heska Emuna Congregation" already has its Temperance Avenue building, whose official address is 502 Vine Avenue, as well as a permanent rabbi, Isaac Winick. The listing shows the immigrants hadn't quite

Rabbi Gary August, who served Temple Beth El as a student rabbi, sometime before World War I. Courtesy of Dr. Harold Winston.

Rabbi Isaac Winick, first rabbi of Heska Amuna, served from 1893 until his death in the early 1920s. Courtesy of Knoxville Jewish Federation.

settled on a permanent English spelling for their *shul*. A board used by the *chevra kadisha* for preparing the dead bears the name "Heska Amono," while an official document seal from that time reads "Congreagation Heska Amona." A gold-handled cane passed down to each synagogue president since 1894 is inscribed with the name "Chesky Amono."

Against this backdrop, the invisible lines between Temple and *Shul* were drawn—Old World versus New World, established affluence versus struggling to get by, the urge to blend in versus the reluctance to be lost in a sea of southern *goyim*. Yet despite all their differences, living as a tiny group of Jews in a small Bible Belt town encouraged fairly cordial relations among Reform and Orthodox children. Around the turn of the century, Knoxville's Jewish teenagers from Temple and *Shul* began a "Junior Jewish Social Club," whose minutes, dated from 1909, still survive in Barbara Winick Bernstein's family collection. Her father, Ben, and Aunt Ida Winick were enthusiastic members and served as officers. The group seems to have been very active socially, though much of its recorded official business dwelled on refreshments for upcoming meetings and fines levied against members for disorderly conduct or talking (reduced, in at least one case, because the offending member claimed he was only whispering, not talking). It was during this time that Temple members Mary and Rose Kate Lippner recall the beginnings of a tradition that has lasted to this day: Every Rosh Hoshana, the Temple's young people attended their own morning services, then walked down Vine Street to the Synagogue to meet their friends. Mrs. Winick, the Orthodox rabbi's wife, always served holiday treats on the front porch, where the young people gathered.

Mrs. Jerome Mark, the wife of the Reform rabbi, even started a Jewish Girl Scout troop, to which Sarah Green and some of her Heska Amuna friends briefly belonged in the early 1920s. The troop, which began with fifteen members, continued throughout the decade under the leadership of Mrs. Mark and later Miss Hermina Beiler of Temple Beth El.

The Sunday school classes of Temple Beth El *(top)* and Heska Amuna Congregation *(bottom)* looked more similar by the 1920s, when the cultural and economic gulf between German Jews and East European Jews was narrowing. The small boy in the foreground of the Heska Amuna class photo is Milton Collins, who would grow up to be the beloved director of Knoxville's Jewish Community Center. Courtesy of Dr. Harold Winston and Knoxville Jewish Federation.

It must have helped that Eastern European Jewish merchants were becoming increasingly involved in the downtown business establishment of Knoxville by the late 1920s. One example was Polish immigrant Max Finklestein, who managed to develop a successful clothing business soon after his arrival in the late 1880s. At the time of his death in 1932, he had erected the Finklestein Building at Gay and Vine and owned or developed numerous other valuable real estate holdings in the downtown area. In addition to being an early president of Heska Amuna and the local B'nai B'rith chapter, Finklestein was a Mason and an Elk and a thirty-second-degree Shriner with a reputation as a great city booster and contributor to charities. (His grandson Zelmore "Steve" Brody and great-granddaughter Pam Branton still live in Knoxville.)

Amid the increasing entry of *Yidden* into middle-class society, the younger people of Temple and Synagogue apparently found themselves more united in the urge to live Jewishly without being too different from Gentile neighbors. Within a generation, that early hard-edged distinction between German and Eastern European Jew had already begun to soften. This trend was occurring all over the South. One cause for the change might have been the increasingly restrictive immigration laws of the 1920s, suggests Carolyn Gray LeMaster in *A Corner of the Tapestry* (University of Arkansas Press, 1994), her history of Arkansas Jews. "With few immigrants to bolster the number of either group, they began to slowly accept each other and intermarry," she notes.

In the forefront of this move to bridge the gap between Knoxville's two Jewish populations was young attorney Ben Winick, the Orthodox rabbi's son and alumnus of the Junior Jewish Social Club. Of course, he had a personal stake in the issue by the early 1920s because he was courting Clara Katz at the Temple. Winick was a man of the New World. Born on American soil in 1897, he graduated from the University of Tennessee law school in 1918 and served with the judge advocate general's corps during World War I. He was one of Rabbi Winick's four sons, all of whom were sports crazy and political. Louis, the eldest, later became a professional boxer, though he fought under a stage name to avoid having his father find out. According to a family story, Louis traveled through Knoxville to fight a bout, which was advertised with posters featuring his picture and the assumed name. Rabbi Winick passed this poster on the street, did a double-take,

Young marrieds Ben and Clara Katz Winick in the late 1920s. Courtesy of Barbara Winick Bernstein.

and came home scratching his head. "Did I see Louis on that poster?" The other brothers hastily assured him it was just a remarkable coincidence. When Louis's fighting career ended, he came back to Knoxville, got a job as a process server, and lived with his widowed mother for the rest of her life. A middle brother, Jacob, died in the flu epidemic of 1918. Brother Frank became a local party politician and justice of the peace. He later allied with Knoxville mayor George Dempster, a man who entered national history as the creator of the Dempster Dumpster. At one point, the local newspaper took to calling their association the "Dempster-Winick Machine." Sister Ida Winick later married Charles Siegel, a long-time Knoxville city councilman and one-time vice mayor.

Ben Winick, the only brother to attend college, was among a small handful of Knoxville Jewish professionals in his generation. (Another was Max Finklestein's son Isadore, who died at a young age.) Winick's papers suggest a man who was passionate about issues, particularly those related to the wave of anti-Semitism and xenophobia sweeping through America in the 1920s. He frequently fired off pointed letters to the editor when something riled him, be it the actions of white supremacist groups or a visiting speaker who blamed the Jews for socialism.

On the local level young Ben Winick turned his considerable zeal toward bringing the two halves of Knoxville Jewry together. In January of 1923, he placed the following notice in the Temple Beth El bulletin:

The Progressive Club

Feeling the need of a center for literary and social activities among the young Jewish men and women of Knoxville, a group of young Jews met at Temple Beth El recently, and decided to organize a club to better carry on the varied activities that should be part of the life of a Jewish community.

In response to the invitation, about sixty young Jewish men and women assembled on the following Sunday and organized the Progressive Club. Various members stressed the point that the new organization should be open to all the young Jews of Knoxville, whether Orthodox or Reform, or whether Synagogue Jew or Temple Jew.

By all showing a whole hearted interest, the Club has grown beyond the fondest dreams of the organizers and much good has already been accomplished at the first few meetings.

We have discovered that the Knoxville Jewish population boasts of varied talents. We abound in real musicians, declaimers, and speakers, and we soon realized that the entire group was interested in literary activities.

Though the Club is very young, a committee has already started plans for a permanent home for the Club, which we hope will be a pride to our city, and in which the entire Jewish population can find a center for every social, athletic and literary activity that intelligent people desire.

Our first social affair was a dance given on Monday night, December 25th, and from the expressions of

Young Jewish Shriners stroll around town in the early 1920s. The younger generation of German and Eastern European Jews mixed freely by this time. *Left to right:* Ben Winick, Dewey Reich, Louis Loef, and Frank Winick. Courtesy of Barbara Winick Bernstein.

guests, it was a decided success. We hope to have many more such affairs in the future, and in this way, the entire Jewish community can cast aside all petty prejudices and work in harmony for what we all desire—a bigger and better Jewish community in a bigger and better Knoxville.

The little club organized by Knoxville Jewish "twenty-somethings" became the direct forerunner of Knoxville's Jewish Community Center. According to Richard Licht, whose father was an early officer of the JCC, Max Arnstein had originally considered donating a social hall building to the Temple. The plan was changed when young Ben Winick paid a formal call on the philanthropist to present a sweeping plan for a center where both Temple and Synagogue Jews could share athletic, social, and cultural activities. (The Center's *Silver Anniversary Book* notes that another source of motivation was Mr. Arnstein's friend Adolph Ochs, who had donated a Jewish community center to Chattanooga a few years earlier. Apparently the two men engaged in a certain amount of friendly competition.) When Arnstein retired in 1929, property was purchased next door to the Temple on Vine Street and a building with a connecting walkway was erected. Whereas other

Jewish communities tend to refer to this common institution as "The JCC" or even "The J," the Knoxville crowd has always called it "the Center." If you had to ask *which* center, you obviously weren't part of the tribe.

Although the Center building's lease was officially held by the Temple until 1954, it immediately became a place where the two crowds mixed freely. Center membership grew throughout the Depression years, even when many families were unable to pay their dues. "After all, nobody could afford to go anywhere or do anything in those years," one longtime resident points out. "So you hung out at the Center to play basketball, meet girls, go to dances, have *simchas* (celebrations)." Even today Knoxville is one of very few communities of its small size to maintain a Jewish community center building. The Arnsteins' commitment was underlined by generous donations over the years, including a large bequest in the 1960s which enabled Knoxville Jews to build the current Arnstein Jewish Community Center on Deane Hill Drive in west Knoxville.

The new Center caused Knoxville Jews to pull together in other ways. In 1930, a joint Temple-Synagogue Sunday school was launched at the Center under the supervision of University of Tennessee agriculture professor William Shaw. Children attended joint sessions on Sunday, which generally focused on cultural knowledge, Jewish history, and holiday celebrations. There was a notably pro-Zionist flavor to the cultural programming, particularly since Dr. Shaw would eventually head the Knoxville Zionist District. The children met together only on Sunday, as Synagogue boys also went to a separate Hebrew school during the week for more instruction, and the Temple later started a Hebrew school of its own. Though parents had to work around tricky issues of *kashrut* (Jewish dietary laws) when bringing in food for children in the joint Sunday school, Dr. Shaw's daughter Genevieve Shaw Kramer remembers it as a time of great cooperation between the two groups. Shaw, of Heska Amuna, was succeeded by Dr. Herbert Nash, of Temple Beth El, who ran the joint Sunday school until 1957. I'm told it was Temple Beth El's Rabbi Solomon Foster who insisted on withdrawing Temple children into a separate Sunday school about 1951, though the Center school continued operation in reduced form for six more years. His motives seem to have more to do with the ever-present turf wars than disagreements over Zionism or Jewish observance. The joint Sunday school alumni—all of whom are now middle-aged to elderly—uniformly insist that it was a big mistake to split up the community's children. For decades the two tiny groups found no way to cooperate in the education of children, until an annual joint conference for teachers was introduced in 1998. Now some combined activities—such as joint Hanukkah parties or Purim

The Knoxville Jewish Community Center, connected by a walkway with Temple Beth El at Vine and Broadway, was common ground for Reform and Orthodox Jews and the hub of Knoxville Jewish life. The building was in use from 1929 to 1969. Courtesy of Dr. Harold Winston.

celebrations—are starting to happen, and a joint high school program is under discussion. Meanwhile, Temple kids and Synagogue kids get to know each other in the Arnstein Jewish Community Center preschool and summer day camp; others meet at the teenage level through the social events of Young Judaea and B'nai B'rith Youth Organization. In between, however, there's very little contact. My children (too old for preschool and too young for BBYO) don't know many of their Jewish peers who pray and learn within walking distance of their own synagogue.

It's ironic. As I write this, in the last months before the year 2000, Temple Jews and Synagogue Jews are probably divided by fewer matters of ritual and belief than ever before. Some decades ago Heska Amuna joined the Conservative movement, which seeks a middle path between the Orthodox and Reform streams of Judaism. Meanwhile, Reform Judaism in America has gradually veered toward more traditional ways. Currently, Rabbi Shlomo Levine of Heska Amuna Synagogue and Rabbi Beth L. Schwartz of Temple Beth El teach a joint class on basic Judaism. The old division between German Jews and Eastern European Jews has long since vanished, replaced by much greater fears that the distinctiveness of Jewish life will vanish into an increasingly secular world. The two institutions are similar in size, and they predominantly include members of equal middle-class affluence. Despite all this—and to the continuing puzzlement of our Christian neighbors, to whom we seem very much the same— our two congregations have continued to be distinct entities. As the old cousins club of related merchant families living near each other has been replaced by unrelated professional families who are spread across the county, the old ties of kinship, business, and physical proximity have loosened as well. "At crunch time this community can be very, very much together," says former Temple Beth El Rabbi Howard Simon, who retired in 1999. "Still, by and large it's probably one of the most independent groups I've ever come up against. Generally speaking, unless there's some kind of major concern, everybody goes their own way." Temple and Synagogue rub along together in the tiny circle of Knoxville Jewish life—as close and yet as separate as the two populations lying to the right and left of that circular drive in the New Jewish Cemetery.

A footnote to this era involves several of the city's more notable Jewish expatriates. Morton Deitch, pictured in 1918 as the only boy in Temple Beth El's first confirmation class, graduated from Yale Law School in 1924, the same year that quotas were first imposed on the university's freshman class to limit the number of incoming Jews. At that time, Jews were rarely hired into Gentile law firms, so competition for the more successful Jewish firms was intense. Fresh out of school, Morton landed a job with Stroock, Stroock, and Lavan, which eventually became one of the most prominent law firms in New York. (The Stroocks in particular were very involved with Jewish cultural and scholarly affairs. A Stroock father and son both served as presidents of the Jewish Theological Seminary, so that from its founding until 1983 every seminary diploma was signed by a Stroock.)

Morton Deitch worked his way up slowly to the inner ring of this small, rarefied circle, which hobnobbed with Warburgs and Supreme Court justices. In 1935 he persuaded his firm to send him to Germany to investigate important documents for a client. This trip involved some peril, as he found himself dealing with minor Nazi officials. His efforts saved the client $100,000, and a year later he was made a partner in Stroock, Stroock, and Lavan. By World War II's onset he was handling some of the firm's most important clients and also making a name for himself as labor relations counsel to Electric Boat Company and the Labor Relations Board. By 1945 day-today management of the firm was in his charge, and he began to be heavily involved in helping to write children's protective legislation for the state of New York. Deitch was prominently identified with the childcare field for more than thirty-five years. He served as chairman of the board of the Jewish Child Care Association of New York and president of the Hillcrest Center for Children, an experimental child care project in Bedford Hills, New York.

Morton Deitch's genteel path upward contrasts sharply with the meteoric rise of Ben Bodne, who appeared briefly on the Knoxville scene. Bodne was an orphan of Eastern European parentage. While still a young man he worked as a porter on railroad cars traveling the South. Each time he would pass through Knoxville, Ben Winick

The Knoxville YMHA basketball champs, 1922. In the front row is Harry Busch, who would grow up to own jewelry and loan offices in Knoxville. In the second row, far left, is Ben Bodne, a poor orphan who would eventually buy New York's Algonquin Hotel. Attorney-to-be Ben Winick is pictured third row, second from the right. Courtesy of Knoxville Jewish Federation.

and his friends would buy the young Bodne a hot meal and take him off to play basketball on their YMHA team. (Bodne is pictured among the young men wearing their Magen David–emblazoned jerseys in the 1920s YMHA photograph above.)

Bodne somehow managed to make a fortune in scrap during World War II. During this period, he and his wife spent an idyllic honeymoon at New York's Algonquin Hotel, home of the famous literary Round Table. Many decades later, Bodne made a romantic gesture: He purchased the financially troubled Algonquin Hotel, reserving for himself a suite of rooms where he lived out his last days, even after he thriftily sold the hotel to a Japanese conglomerate. Barbara Bernstein remembers visiting him there when she was a newlywed living in New York in the 1950s. It seems he always fondly remembered those long-ago basketball games in Knoxville.

A third Knoxville Jewish expatriate is remembered primarily for a postmortem act of generosity to his hometown. Frank Dryzer was the child of Eastern European immigrants who ran a tiny grocery on the corner of Union and South Central and lived over the store. He studied Hebrew with Rabbi Isaac Winick, helped out at the store, and somehow managed to win the 1905 University of Tennessee Junior Faculty Fellowship for excellence in schoolwork. His parents managed to scrape up the rest of the funds to send Frank and his brother Max through college. Max became a successful wholesale shoe jobber in New York. Frank, who had "piercing black eyes that could look right through you," according to another community member, was a math genius who also did a thesis on the Roman emperor Nero, complete with Latin translations. He was the quiet type and never married. After a brief stint teaching at Girls High in Knoxville, Dryzer took a job in the Patent Office in Washington, D.C., where he stayed until his death at sixty-four. However, he never forgot what it meant to be a needy student. Dryzer's will left $50,000—a substantial bequest in the late 1940s—to establish fellowships at his alma mater, the University of Tennessee. ∞

Four

Family *A*ffairs

otes, June 7, 1998. My original plan was to make a comprehensive multi-family tree that charted the tight little universe of Knoxville-area Jews. I've given up this tidy notion, falling back on various scraps of notebook paper scrawled with lines and arrows. There is no good way to keep track of all the siblings, uncles, great-aunts, in-laws, and second-cousins-twice-removed who show up in the stories people tell around here. Each time I try to sort out the question of who's related to whom in this community, the strands of kinship look as tangled as one of those lumpy plastic lanyards I used to make in summer camp.

Still, the names are getting familiar now. I could tell you how the fairly sizable Robinson-Green-Reback-Gluck-Diftler-Slovis clan hooks up by marriage with the Millen-Abrams-Levison-Brown-Shersky tribe but not the Sturm-Balloff-Hasden-Landis-Abeles families. I haven't yet figured out if these strands join with the even more complex Friedman-Fay-Fayonsky-Smullian-Hahn-Billig-Schwarzbart-Morrison-Joffe-Shaw-Kramer-Ross line. No doubt someone reading this page will probably explain it to me later with that air of amused exasperation the older generation of Knoxville Jews reserves for nouveau greenhorns like myself. When they were growing up, no one needed to ask such questions. They could (and still do) argue over the specific geometry of connection, but in those days, being a member of the community literally meant you were *family.* "Yeah, tell me about it," laughed a middle-aged woman seated next to me at a recent Knoxville Jewish Federation fund-raiser. "When I first moved to this town thirty years ago, people warned me, 'Never say anything nasty about anyone, because you're probably talking to her cousin.' They're all related to each other."

This is perhaps the most typical of patterns for a small Jewish community, particularly in the South. Historians credit much of this interconnectedness to "chain migration," the process by which one member of an immigrant family settles in an area and gradually brings over a wife and children, a nephew, some cousins. One relative finds employment in his uncle's shop, then starts a related business and puts out the word to his cousins that business opportunity is good. Relatives lend each other money for new ventures and partnerships are formed. The children of one clan marry into another, further tightening the bonds of kinship, business partnership, and mutual dependence.

I marvel at how radically this situation has changed in only three decades. Most of the Jewish householders currently living in East Tennessee are now unrelated professional people who were drawn to the area by jobs (often in the university, TVA, the Oak Ridge National Laboratory, or one of the local hospitals). Most of *their* children grow up, go off to college, and settle elsewhere, though our population grows slowly as other people's children take jobs here. That's a common story in cities all over America, as Jews have followed jobs. Particularly in the South, economic forces undercut the old Jewish businesses just as southern universities, research institutions, and retirement communities embarked upon major expansion. The children of the old merchant clans drifted away, almost completely replaced by an unrelated population of Jewish professionals and retirees. According to historian Leonard Dinnerstein, more than 80 percent of today's southern Jews do not originally hail from this region.

Here, as elsewhere, it is quite unlikely that our community ever again will be organized primarily around kinship. Yet somehow the cousins club that used to be so dominant is still clearly a part of our communal rhythm, orchestrating the many ways we deal with one another. "Sometimes this community is like a weird, overgrown, somewhat dysfunctional family," is the fond comment of Rabbi Arthur Weiner, a New York City native who served Heska Amuna from 1989 to 1996. He is now rabbi for the Jewish Community Center of Paramus, New Jersey, where he lives in a county that contains more than 100,000 Jews, fifty synagogues, and three kosher restaurants. By contrast, Knoxville has fewer than 2,000 Jews, two synagogues, and one deli where you can get a kosher meal on paper plates if you ask for it. "Yet in a city with so few Jewish institutions, people really pour their hearts and souls into what they have," Rabbi Weiner says. "When I first came to Knoxville—as a twenty-eight-year-old seminary graduate, knowing very little about the South—I was surprised at how much ability people had to lead services and read Torah. This is a community that has conducted its own ritual life for decades! Plus, in Knoxville, the Synagogue is an extension of home and family. People can get very angry with each other and storm off. But after a while they usually return, and hardly anyone ever quits the *shul*. Where would they go? It would be like leaving your family. The basic attitude is that nobody's expendable."

Notes, October 1, 1998. At times, the early imprint of that East Tennessee cousins club can show up in some charming ways. Yesterday was Yom Kippur. At Heska Amuna, the first long service ends in the early afternoon, at which point most people go home for a leisurely nap to ease the rigors of fasting. Forty or fifty hardy souls regroup in the late afternoon for an informal lecture-discussion. Then by twilight everybody else is straggling in to resume services, which act as a sort of preamble to the beautiful Neilah, or "gateway," prayers at the close of Yom Kippur. Before Neilah, a portion of Torah (five books of Moses) is read and a Haftorah (section from the prophetic books of the Bible) is recited. All this is done in Hebrew, of course, using the "trope" or prescribed musical notes assigned to each line of text according to an unbroken tradition that stretches back thousands of years. Reciting a Haftorah and accompanying blessings in front of the congregation is a challenging task which often forms the centerpiece accomplishment of a child becoming bar or bat mitzvah at age thirteen. For three generations now, the *aliyah* (formal honor) of reciting the Haftorah at this particular point on Yom Kippur has usually fallen to a member of the Robinson family. This year, it was a thrill to watch ten-year-old Eli

Robinson, a member of the fourth generation, get up to share part of the Haftorah with his father, Pace, in the company of his grandfather Mitchell. I heard later that it was Eli's own idea to study for this difficult task. Even for the youngest Robinsons, Jewish learning and family tradition are tightly intertwined.

We've already met Eli's great-great aunt Sarah Green Robinson. She was married at age eighteen to Nathan, one of six Robinson brothers who came from Russia before World War I. Like so many Jewish men, the six Robinson boys shipped out to America in order to avoid the brutal fate of conscription into the Russian army. Jews were required to serve many years longer than Christians and often didn't survive the experience. Avoiding this service was often a matter of stiff bribes to officials, forged papers, and great personal risk to the families. Sarah tells me her husband, Nathan, just barely escaped, having to hide several times along the way from various army recruitment gangs. Three other brothers—Sam (called S. H.), Morris (called M. B.) and Max—were already in Knoxville. Another, Frank, was killed in a buggy accident. In those days, the usual reason that a Jew came to Knoxville was to work for a relative who already had a business here. Others were drawn to settle near a *landsmann*—someone from the home village in Europe. The Robinson brothers came because an uncle named B. J. Thorpe had developed a thriving junk business in the Vine Street area. However, it didn't take these young men long to find other opportunities. S. H. opened a feed store, while the other brothers sold junk, appliances, and secondhand goods.

Knoxville in the 1920s was a thriving urban manufacturing center, one of the biggest mill towns in the South. The very contours of the city were beginning to change rapidly. At the turn of the century, Knoxville's borders enclosed a compact little urban grid that could easily be walked from one end to the other in less than two hours. A series of annexations in 1917 suddenly increased Knoxville's land area to five times its previous size, adding huge new suburban tracts that could only be reached by streetcar or motor vehicle. Unsurprisingly, car sales were booming by the mid-1920s. Taking note of this trend, Nathan Robinson opened a used auto parts company about the same

Left: Sarah Green Robinson, mid-1930s. *Below:* Sarah and Nathan Robinson with their children on a family trip to Bristol, Tennessee, 1931. Courtesy of Joyce Robinson Diftler.

time he married Sarah. Their union was arranged in a quaintly Old World fashion: S. H. spoke to Sarah's father after morning prayers at the *shul* one day, mentioning that all the brothers thought it was high time for their youngest, twenty-nine-year-old Nathan, to be married. Didn't Joe Green have a teenage daughter at home? S. H. wondered aloud. Joe then checked it out with his wife and daughter, who consented to let Nathan come calling. Still, Sarah was an American-born girl of the emancipated 1920s. She immediately learned to drive and scandalized her sisters-in-law by jaunting down to the noisy, dirty auto yard each day to handle Nathan's bookkeeping.

The last Robinson brother to arrive was Eli and Asher's great-grandfather Avraham Jehuda (known as A. J.), the eldest as well as the family's primary Torah scholar. He originally settled in Providence as a Hebrew teacher but came to Knoxville when the other brothers arranged a twenty-five-dollar-per-week job as Heska Amuna's kosher butcher/*kashrut* inspector. In the traditional way, the other Robinsons felt a responsibility to help their more learned brother financially so he could continue studying and provide ritual services for the community. They bought him a small grocery store/deli on Vine Street so A. J. could piece together a living. "My father made good pickles, and he used to go watch Lippner [whose butcher stall in the Market House had kosher and nonkosher sides] to make sure he was doing it right," relates his oldest son Mitchell. The backyard of the deli contained chicken coops where A. J. butchered fresh chicken according to strict *kashrut.* Sometimes local women would bring him their own live birds. ("When the pigeons on our windowsill became a nuisance, my mother used to set traps, then take them down to A. J. Robinson for slaughtering so we could taste this special treat," recalls Genevieve Shaw Kramer.) Mitchell still remembers how his father would mark such bills "15 cents P & K" for "plucking and killing."

At the end of World War I, the brothers sent Max back to Lithuania in order to search for their widowed mother amid the tumult of the Bolshevik Revolution. When he finally found her, half-starved in the basement of a ruined building, he nursed her back to health for three months and then returned with her to Knoxville. (For the record, this actually makes Eli and his younger brother, Asher, the

In the early 1920s, a growing Heska Amuna Congregation moved to a new synagogue building on Fifth Avenue. Courtesy of Barbara Winick Bernstein.

fifth generation of Robinsons to live here. They are also fifth-generation Knoxville Jews by way of their grandmother Natalie Levison Robinson, whose family story we'll get to in a bit.)

Eli and Asher's grandfather Mitchell Robinson was born in 1924, exactly nine months after family friends arranged a match for the forty-two-year-old A. J. with a woman twenty years younger. His bride was the feisty Sylvia Auerbach Robinson, who had come to America as a teenager with her two brothers. She went to work in clothing factories, at one time served as a union organizer, and eventually saved up enough to bring over her parents. One day, a cousin brought A. J. over to the family apartment. "I was up a ladder washing windows for *yontiff* [a holiday celebration], and he took one look and that was it," Sylvia Robinson recalled sixty years later in a taped interview by Barbara Bernstein and Natalie Robinson. "A. J. wouldn't quit till I married him." The newlyweds moved directly to Knoxville, settling on North Fourth Street in what was gradually becoming a cluster of Jewish merchant families. This area, located a few blocks from the downtown business district, represented a step up from the boardinghouses and crowded above-the-store lodgings along Vine Street, where the earlier generation of Jews had settled. The "Fourth and Gill" neighborhood was full of late-Victorian clapboard houses, with backyards big enough for keeping animals and front porches wide enough to chat with neighbors on a summer evening. Almost immediately, A. J.'s mother, Frieda, moved in with them, where she stayed until her death nineteen years later. "She was a real old-fashioned Jewish lady, about four and a half feet high, and all her big, tall sons just treated her like a queen," Sylvia later recalled with wry humor. "Me—I was just lately come from Europe and I didn't know better, so they took advantage." For several years, young marrieds Sarah and Nathan moved to the upper floors of the big house and, as babies arrived, it was filled with the ruckus of three generations. The pattern was a good one, Sylvia admitted later, for in her old age her own sons treated her "like a queen."

Everybody got along pretty well until 1930, when A. J.'s deal with the Synagogue provoked a divisive split in the Orthodox congregation. It was the only time in its history that the "overgrown family" actually came to a physical parting of the ways. The main issue seemed to be that some community leaders wanted to discontinue A. J.'s monthly retainer as a *schochet,* or kosher butcher, while others were outraged at such a departure from tradition. Several younger families in the breakaway group also wanted some progressive reforms, such as making full Hebrew education available to girls. The conflict grew heated. Finally, about sixty people—including the many-branched Green and Robinson families as well as six Slovis brothers (who ran a string of pawn shops)—broke away to form their own small shul, called Beth Israel. It was housed in a large upstairs room at 133½ Gay Street, partly above Billig's Kosher Restaurant. The area has since been overhauled, but the little shul stood very close to the spot on Gay Street now occupied by Harold Shersky's Kosher-Style Food Center. (Mitchell Robinson later enjoyed telling people he was "bar-mitzvahed upstairs from Harold's Deli.") "Back in those days, we called it 'the pawnbrokers *shul*' because a number of families who ran pawn shops belonged there," recalls Joe Billig, son of restaurant owners Louis and Betty Billig. "Of course, being in the kosher food business, our family had to belong to both *shuls*!"

University of Tennessee agriculture professor William Shaw, who was then supervisor of the joint religious school, brought his family to the new synagogue. "It was a wonderful little *shul*," says his daughter Genevieve Shaw Kramer (who would later become Joe Billig's sister-in-law). Congregation Beth Israel hired a young, charismatic rabbi named Israel Levine, who introduced Modern Orthodox innovations such as Hebrew training for girls and "Junior Congregation" services led by youngsters. "It was in Rabbi Levine's Hebrew classes that we spent mornings of our summer vacation—since there were no Jewish day camps—and we also attended two afternoons a week during the school year," says Genevieve. Five years later, when Rabbi Levine moved on to another pulpit, Beth Israel's families finally rejoined Heska Amuna, bringing along some innovations that still survive. Today, boys and girls receive identical Hebrew training and "Junior Congregation" is still the forum in which young people learn to conduct services. (Fittingly, perhaps, these "Junior Cong" youth services are held in the small chapel dedicated to the memory of the Rev. A. J. and Sylvia Robinson.)

A. J., Sylvia, and infant Mitchell Robinson. Courtesy of Mitchell and Natalie Robinson.

When A. J.'s son Mitchell married Natalie Levison two decades later, the Robinson and Green clans were linked with three other branches of the old family network—the Millens, Levisons, and Coplans. Natalie's maternal grandfather, Isaac Coplan, was a signatory of the original Heska Amuna charter in 1890. He first lived in Dosset near present-day Oak Ridge before opening a well-known grocery store called Coplan's Corner on University and Fifth. Around the same time, Natalie's paternal grandfather, Nathan Levison, had a thriving business selling lumber for railroad construction around the Guggenheim-owned mining camps near Ducktown (best known more than a century later as the site of kayaking competitions at a recent Summer Olympic Games). Natalie's father, Hyman, was born in one of the area's mining camps in 1895. Nathan bought a large piece of timbered land, which was immediately dubbed "Jew Field" by local residents. It seems to have retained that distinctive name for many decades after his sudden demise in the early 1890s. Kicked in the head by a horse, Nathan was brought to Knoxville for medical treatment and became one of the first burials in the New Jewish Cemetery off Middlebrook Pike. The widowed Fanny Millen Levison chose to stay in Knoxville, where she had seven brothers and sisters. To support Hyman and her three other children, Fanny opened a kosher boardinghouse, which catered primarily to the many immigrant Jewish peddlers who came over from Europe without their families. "It was incredibly popular because everybody loved Fanny's cooking," recalled her niece, the late Babe Millen Fay, in a taped interview. Eventually, a bachelor peddler named Max Taylor parked his horse and buggy at Fanny's door. She married him and had another child.

After military service during World War I, Fanny's son Hyman went off to open a chain of ladies shoe stores in Bristol, Tennessee, where he was a charter member of the tiny synagogue in Bristol, Virginia–Tennessee. As early as 1904, a handful of Jewish merchants began meeting for religious services in the isolated, mountainous Tri-Cities area (formed by Johnson City, Tennessee; Kingsport, Tennessee; and Bristol, which lies across the Virginia–Tennessee border). The little congregation, called B'nai Sholom (Children of Peace), followed the pattern of many tiny Southern communities in bringing together Germans and Eastern Europeans, Reform and Orthodox Jews, in an often uneasy alliance. (Tellingly, a large number of such congregations contained the word *sholom* or *shalom* ["peace"] in their names.) By 1905 the community had purchased land for a burial ground, and in 1919 it managed to hire a *shokhet,* or ritual butcher, who could provide kosher meat as well as lead worship services and provide some Hebrew instruction to the children. The community also included active Zionists in a B'nai Zion Society, even managing to send a representative to the 1917 state Zionist convention in Nashville.

Hyman Levison's name appears with that of Isaac Levine, Joseph Strauss, and Ralph Gourse on a 1927 letter announcing the purchase of a synagogue by a "membership of twelve," who solicited others to "help us in our unselfish undertaking to establish Jewish

Ideals and Jewish Citizenship in our small town." A scribbled post-script adds, "It will take about $6000 to put us out of debt." Hyman lived in Bristol for some years but eventually moved to Atlanta, where Natalie and her brothers, Gilbert and Jarvin, were raised.

(We pause now for a genealogical fast-forward. The aforementioned Babe Fay, born Babe Millen, was the mother of Jan Fay, a Heska Amuna member whose "Fay Portable Buildings" are now ubiquitous on construction sites and outdoor events all over town. In the late 1940s, plump, maternal Babe Fay prevailed on that dashing war veteran Mitchell Robinson to take out her stylish young cousin Natalie, who had just arrived in town to take a job at her uncle's downtown clothing store. Thus—due to Babe Fay's matchmaking efforts—at least three of those long strings of family names mentioned in the first paragraph of this chapter *are* related in one way or another. At least, I *think* so.)

Babe Millen Fay's memories of growing up Jewish in Knoxville paint a picture of many small, interrelated merchant families, each scraping by with a small store where goods were sold or repaired or peddled secondhand. This was the way of smaller towns throughout the South, where very few Jews had large businesses and very few held working-class jobs. ("When I took my children on trips to Atlanta and such, they were always surprised to see Jews doing things like delivering milk or driving a truck," Sarah Robinson chuckles. "In Knoxville, nearly every Jew owned a shop or at least worked for relatives.") Shoes, clothing, groceries, jewelry, and junk were the main Jewish businesses in the 1920s and 1930s, and almost all were located in a close walking area around Vine, Central, Gay, and Market Streets. According to newspaper reports from that era, the entire Jewish community numbered only about six hundred, perched in a city of 150,000 Gentiles. Babe Fay recalled: "As a young girl, I went to McMillan School on Church Street . The first time I walked in the classroom, all the children had their heads bowed down on the desk. They were praying, but I thought they were crying. So I sat down and cried along with them."

She also remembered the simple but joyous celebrations within the Jewish community, surrounded by her many uncles and cousins. "On Simchas Torah [the very joyous fall festival that celebrates the end and beginning of the annual cycle of reading Torah] my uncle

Sam Millen would paint sweet potatoes with black shoe polish, bore a hole in the top for a candle, and put each one on a stick. We kids would march around with lighted candles, singing 'ah-nay-nu, ah-nay-nu' [part of the traditional verses of celebration]. I'm walking around doing 'ah-nay-nu' and my friend Ida Tobe gets a little too close behind me. Next thing I know, my hair's on fire!"

Another richly detailed view of Knoxville Jewish life in the 1920s and 30s comes from Genevieve Shaw Kramer, who marked her seventieth birthday by compiling a family history for her children and grand-children. She used numerous public and personal sources, including the meticulous accounting records kept by her father, University of Tennessee agriculture professor William Shaw. The result was an open letter to her children about the people she calls "Bubbie" and "Zadie" (Yiddish for Grandma and Grandpa). In 1910, twenty-one-year-old William Shaw left his home in the Ukraine with the help of an underground Jewish group and a fake visa. He made his way to Holland, boarded a boat to Nova Scotia, and came to St. Paul, Minnesota, where some cousins had already settled. He took on the surname "Shaw" used by these cousins and immediately looked for ways to further his education. He was too old to earn a public high school diploma, so he studied at the public library while working as a short-order cook in a diner. A kindly librarian he met there sponsored his admission to a private boy's academy, from which he was graduated six months later as valedictorian. Shaw went on to study soil chemistry at the University of Minnesota, where he earned bachelor's and master's degrees. In 1920 (three years after marrying Celia Berkovitz), Shaw was recruited for the extension program at the University of Tennessee's new School of Agriculture, together with his fellow classmate Simon Marcovitch. Both men and their wives were destined to play important roles in the Knoxville Jewish community. (In fact, I feel particularly indebted to Simon Marcovitch's wife, Anne, who wrote a detailed history of the Jewish community for Temple Beth El's eightieth anniversary celebration.)

Throughout the 1920s and 1930s, the Shaw family struggled financially on the modest salary of a University of Tennessee agriculture professor, partly because of high medical bills for Mrs. Shaw and their son, Milton. William Shaw's neat little account book for 1933 records a payment of $165 for Milton's mastoid surgery to deal with recurrent ear problems. Genevieve recalls "sitting in the waiting room of Dr. Reaves's infirmary, hearing the horrible sounds of a chisel used to reach the infection behind the bone." Dr. Reaves was paid over a period of two years, sometimes only five dollars a month. Meanwhile, Mrs. Shaw was frequently ill. She later confided that her own decision to become "Shomer Shabbat"—a strict observer of Jewish law regarding Shabbat, holidays, and other customs—was made in a private vow after doctors told her she would never live to raise her youngest child, Genevieve. "I recall when I was in the second grade, my teacher, Miss Prater, a devout Christian who required us to kneel in prayer every day after lunch, heard of Bubbie's illness and invited herself to our home," writes Genevieve. "She then offered to adopt me since she thought I might be orphaned." Genevieve still recalls the serious, courteous expressions with which the two elder Shaws listened to the teacher's proposal, though it must have seemed the height of absurdity to a pair of observant Jews.

"A memory that stands out during the periods when Bubbie was ill and unable to care for us is the hippolite sandwiches," Genevieve continues. "Zadie concluded that hippolite (egg-white marshmallow whip) was something we would like and we could easily prepare as a tasty and nourishing sandwich. This was the days before peanut butter. He would buy hippolite by the case and instruct us to eat all the hippolite sandwiches we wanted." Still, the family managed to send money to "Jewish relief" and overseas relatives in need. During the Depression, the family charged groceries at a local grocery store and paid the bill monthly. Every Friday, Celia Shaw would ask the grocer to add one dollar to their bill and give her that one dollar in cash. She then came home and wrote her mother a weekly letter, enclosing the one-dollar bill.

In 1930, the Shaw family relocated from the university area to a comfortable brick home in the Fourth and Gill neighborhood, where so many Jews now lived. "A deed was recorded for $1 cash and a personal note for $275, plus two mortgages, all adding up to $4,000," Genevieve recalls. "We could walk to Heska Amuna Synagogue [which relocated to Fifth Avenue in the 1920s] and share holiday observances in the neighborhood. Our house was always a center of activity. In spite of her poor health, Bubbie always managed to serve delicious goodies on her beautiful white linen cloths." As the Depression worsened, many of the fine old homes of the neighborhood were subdivided for rental income, a process that eventually led to the area's decline. Genevieve's own parents slept in a curtained-off area of the dining room in order that one or two upstairs bedrooms could be rented out to single Jewish boarders. She particularly remembers one boarder, a violin teacher named Mr. Mendelson, who parked his car in a detached garage they had out back. Genevieve and her brother Milton were raising baby chicks in the same garage, and Milton set up a kerosene heater to keep them warm. One day when everyone was gone, the chicks overturned the heater and burned down the whole garage, including Mr. Mendelson's car. "We accepted our blame," Genevieve says cryptically.

Summer vacations were spent doing home improvement projects. The handy William Shaw dug out the basement to install an extra bathroom and put in a large copper boiler, where his wife could boil her sheets to pristine whiteness. Genevieve remembers that the basement also held her father's large worktable. "One of my most vivid memories is learning how to open fresh-killed chickens on that table. Bubbie would not trust the local butcher, since she wanted to check for blemishes [which would have rendered the chicken *tref* (unclean)]." Over the years, the industrious Professor Shaw was able to provide his children with small luxuries—piano lessons for Genevieve, violin lessons for her older sister Ruth taught by Barbara Bernstein's mother Clara Katz, even tickets to the Mickey Mouse Club held on weekends at the Tennessee Theater. (The observant Genevieve Shaw and her friends bought their tickets for the Saturday Mickey Mouse event the day before, in order to avoid handling money on the Sabbath. However, Genevieve remembers that Rabbi Levine once took them aside and gently suggested that the Holy One wouldn't find this a very good use of Shabbes. Virtue triumphed in the reluctant girls, who gave up their Saturday treat.)

Social life revolved around this tiny but vibrant Jewish circle. William and Celia Shaw participated in a Sunday evening small-stakes poker game that rotated between the homes of five Jewish couples for a period of about fifteen years. (He was so organized that weekly wins and losses were duly recorded under the categories "self" and "wife.") Still, his account book shows that continuing medical bills forced him to borrow sums from various friends in town, including his colleague Simon Marcovitch and jeweler Max Friedman.

Today's Jewish Knoxville is almost uniformly middle class to upper middle class. It isn't easy to imagine the Depression years, when hungry and homeless Jews drifted through town while established families drifted away in search of jobs. (There's a poignant notation in the minutes of the Knoxville Hadassah chapter for January 17, 1931: "A motion was made by Mrs. M. Reamer, seconded by Mrs. A. Slovis and carried, that we drop out of the [Southern] Region, in view of losing all our funds in the Bank failure, and also notifying them that when we are financially able, we will rejoin them.") The tiny shul in Bristol was repeatedly threatened with mortgage foreclosure. For seven years, synagogue leaders Ralph Gourse, Tom Green, and Uel Ross struggled to pay the bills and argued with bankers to get extensions.

Knoxville Jews in the grocery business often extended long-term credit to members of the community. After the death of grocer Ben Goodstein, who ran a store on Luttrell Street, his son Joe found seven boxes of outstanding IOUs, many written in Yiddish and dating back to the 1930s. (Even in the depths of the Depression, Goodstein's store was a central gathering spot for Orthodox housewives on Friday morning, after cattle had been slaughtered and prepared to conform with proper kashrut. Joe remembers that "old Mrs. Slovis" would invariably plant herself down on a large bag of beans to direct traffic among the "yiddische mamas" impatiently waiting for their Shabbos meat orders. Some years later, Mrs. Slovis lay ill in a hospital room, where a crucifix with the body of Jesus was displayed prominently on the wall. A Jewish friend visiting her asked if she wanted to have the crucifix taken down. "No, leave it," replied Mrs. Slovis. "He's also a *landsmann.*")

In a community so tied up in the bonds of *landsmannskeit* and kinship, it isn't surprising that people would feel deeply bound by the Jewish duty of *tzedakah*—righteous acts toward the less fortunate. The

Orthodox *rebbetsin* Mrs. Winick was famous for doling out small sums from her apron pocket during the early days. Later on, Max Friedman from the Synagogue and Dewey Reich from the Temple made generous gifts and loans to dozens of families. Reich is also credited with starting a modest program to disperse funds to transient Jews through the new Jewish Community Center. It wouldn't be too great a stretch to call this effort the earliest forerunner of today's Knoxville Jewish Federation, which operates a variety of scholarship and grant programs including a transient fund. During the past decade—roughly a century after the Knoxville Ladies Hebrew Benevolent Auxiliary collected funds for East European immigrants—the Knoxville Jewish Federation organized the resettlement of several dozen families from the former Soviet Union in this area.

Toward the end of the Depression, Celia Shaw often combined forces with her card-playing partner Mrs. Oscar Glazer, the matriarch of a growing scrap iron business. The setup was very basic: Discovering a need in the community, Mrs. Shaw would call Mrs. Glazer, who was adept at vigorously collecting funds among the downtown merchants. The immigrant Ida Glazer knew from personal experience how quickly a family's fortunes could rise and fall. Her husband, Oscar Glazer, had immigrated to America in the early years of the century and sent for his family shortly before World War I. The Glazers originally settled in Atlanta but left there after the 1915 lynching of Jewish factory manager Leo Frank, an event which sent ripples of fear through Jewish communities all over the South. (Leo Frank, falsely accused of killing a thirteen-year-old girl employed in the plant, was convicted amid a sensational trial. Anti-Semitic rhetoric ran high during the trial, and many Jews feared violent reprisals. When Frank's sentence was commuted, a mob kidnapped him from the prison farm where he was being held and lynched him. So virulent was the sentiment against him, writes Leonard Dinnerstein in *The Leo Frank Case*, that hundreds purchased photos of the corpse and pieces of the lynching rope as souvenirs. It is no wonder that the incident left southern Jews, particularly in the Deep South, with a profound sense of insecurity that lingered for decades.)

It was against this backdrop that Oscar (a.k.a. Aaron) Glazer set out from Atlanta in a horse and carriage to find a safe haven for his growing family. In Knoxville he found a *landsmann*, a fellow immigrant from his Russian hometown. It seemed a good sign that numerous Knoxville Jews had successful businesses in the downtown area and were actively involved in local affairs. Things seemed pretty quiet. Glazer opened a small grocery store in the Old City but lost all his possessions in a 1916 bank panic. "My mother had to borrow a nickel to buy soap to wash clothes," says his daughter Gert Glazer Cohen. She recalls standing at the corner of Clinch and Gay Street with her father, watching people shake the doors of the bank as they desperately tried to get their money back. Luckily for Oscar, America's 1917 entry into World War I created an urgent need for metals. He took his horse and buggy and traveled around the countryside of Tennessee and Kentucky buying scrap iron for shipment north to mills in Ohio. Conditions were hazardous. One family story relates that Oscar was stopped one day by a southern sheriff who demanded to see his business license on pain of imprisonment in the local jail. In fact, Glazer's license was actually in the name of a cousin with a different name. He took a deep breath and brandished the document in front of the sheriff. "See, it says G-L-A-Z-E-R," he told the illiterate sheriff, who nodded importantly and let him pass. (A similar story about Glazer's contemporary, Fred Millen, was related to me by Mitchell Robinson. It seems Millen was approached by a sheriff who demanded to see his peddling license. Having none, Millen pulled out his pocket watch and announced in broken English, "A quarter to two, sir!" Every time the sheriff asked, Millen looked at his watch and gave the same sincere response, until the sheriff gave up in frustration.)

Oscar Glazer kept the Jewish dietary laws as he traveled, living on egg-and-sardine sandwiches all week until he could get home to his wife's kosher table for Shabbat dinner. He frequently stopped in to visit Jews in surrounding areas, often selling memberships in Heska Amuna or collecting much-needed dues. His own business flourished in the 1920s, allowing him enough profit to buy a new Model-T Ford. Then it all disappeared in the stock market crash of 1929. What did it take, I wonder, to keep starting over? Who helped him? The record shows that during the middle years of the Depression, Glazer managed to start a downtown scrap yard called Glazer Iron and Steel. His six children all helped out after school, weighing scrap on the big scales, typing letters, and doing the books.

When Oscar Glazer died suddenly in 1939, his European-born spouse—who until that point had been strictly a housewife—learned to drive a car and took over control of the business. It struggled along until her daughter Gert married Buddy Cohen, a short, scrappy young man from the streets of New York who was sent to visit relatives in Knoxville because he'd fallen in with tough companions and would probably end up dead or in jail. Once married, however, Buddy poured his energies into Glazer Steel, which boomed with the need for scrap metals during World War II. For a time, the Glazer-Cohen tribe was one of the wealthiest Jewish families in Knoxville.

Notes, June 23, 1999. Brad Sturm, may his memory be a blessing, was buried today. He was only forty-three, the victim of a sudden heart attack. We are all so stunned, so immensely saddened by the loss of this man in his prime, one of the last of Knoxville's Jewish merchants, a devoted husband, and the father of two young sons. Rabbi Arthur and Shira Weiner, who were close friends of the Sturms, came down from New Jersey. Victor Rashkovsky (rabbi of the Oak Ridge congregation, where Brad grew up) cut short his vacation to fly home. So many hundreds of people from Knoxville and Oak Ridge came to the funeral that they literally had to line up along the walls of the big sanctuary. Even on Yom Kippur I never saw the synagogue so crowded. "Brad was not a man given to hobbies," said Arthur Weiner, whose voice broke often as he delivered Brad's eulogy. "He pursued his business vigorously, and the rest of his time he gave to his family." Heads nodded all over the room; tears flowed. Bradley Sturm was happily enmeshed in a great web of family. Sturms have lived in this area since before World War I, and their relatives are legion. Just a few weeks before his death, he spent thirty minutes on the phone with me, explaining how the intricacies of local kinship surrounded him and his wife, the former Melissa Hasden. "At one point, my grandmother Sturm and my great-aunt, Esther Balloff, were both living in this small four-unit apartment house in the Sequoyah Hills neighborhood," Brad told me. Next door lived Alice Landis, and in the next building over was yet another Jewish woman, who was kin to her by marriage. "So then I married Melissa [Hasden], who is Alice's granddaughter. Instantly, all these four ladies living in the same place became related to each other. They got such a big kick out of that."

Some months before, I had talked for several hours to Brad's father, retired Oak Ridge businessman Mel Sturm, and listened to a taped interview with Mel's aunt, the late Esther Sturm Balloff. In many ways, their family story paints a classic portrait of the small Jewish merchant clans who established businesses in the rural South and became central figures in those communities.

As Esther told it, the first Sturms came to America from Rumania in 1883, settling in New York the same year the Brooklyn Bridge was opened. Her father ran a series of small restaurants on the Lower East Side, Washington Heights, and finally Brooklyn. Esther was raised in this intensely Jewish world until she was in her teens. Everything changed in 1916 when Esther went to visit her favorite aunt in Pineville, Kentucky. A small number of merchant Jews had settled in the coal towns of Pineville and nearby Middlesboro, where they catered to a population of coal miners and railroad construction workers. During Esther's visit, a terrible epidemic broke out in New York. Her aunt refused to let her leave and eventually convinced Esther's whole family to join them in Kentucky. "I cried for a week," Esther recalled later, "I already had boyfriends back in New York."

About this time, the enterprising Louis Balloff moved to Middlesboro to work for the Ginzberg family clothing business. He and Esther were married three years later. Rabbi Isaac Winick came up from Knoxville to perform the wedding, bringing along his own salami to eat because the Pineville Jews were unable to get kosher meat. "The whole thing was in Hebrew," Esther later remarked archly. "The rabbi didn't ask me anything and I didn't have to promise anything." Like many Jewish women of her generation, she spoke fluent Yiddish but could understand little Hebrew. Later, Rabbi Winick also came to perform the *bris*, or circumcision ceremony, for each of Esther's sons. In those days, he served as a kind of circuit-riding *mohel*, performing circumcisions for Jews in all outlying areas. In Barbara

Esther Sturm Balloff
(left) poses in 1920 with
her parents, Henry and
Eva Sturm, and her
sister-in-law Beatrice
Cawn Sturm. Courtesy
of Mel and Fran Sturm.

Bernstein's copious files, I saw a letter from a local doctor who had
observed Winick's procedures and certified that he performed such
surgeries "with Haste and Care, resulting well."

The newlywed Balloffs moved to La Follette, a country town
near the northern border of Tennessee. Louis started a clothing store,
which did well almost immediately. For the next four years, they were
the only Jews in town. It was a tolerant place, Esther recalled later.
They were always treated like full members of the little community.
"I brought my matzah to the restaurant on Passover," she recalled
with a chuckle. For many years, Louis was a fixture in the little drugstore on the town's main street, where he used to read his Yiddish
newspaper every morning. It is notable that the Balloffs felt this level
of acceptance among their Bible Belt neighbors at a time when Jews

in southern cities—including Knoxville—were frequently excluded from the higher rungs of Gentile society. The simplest answer is that small towns such as La Follette didn't have enough social rungs to bother with such exclusions. Deborah Weiner at the University of West Virginia notes the same sort of "fluid social dynamics" during this era in her profile of a small West Virginia coal town, "The Jews of Keystone" for *Southern Jewish History.* "Jews played an active role in Keystone social life," writes Weiner. "They developed close friendships with non-Jews, both black and white, who occupied the same socioeconomic position. They participated in fraternal clubs as members and leaders."

Indeed, any family who owned a major store filled a natural leadership position in a small, poor town such as La Follette. By 1920 the depleted coal mines closed up, leaving many destitute. Miners and other service workers were left with near-useless scrip as their wages. Louis Balloff took the paper at discount and returned cash, allowing many people to buy food and clothing, Esther recalls. "Afterwards people came to us and said, 'Mrs. Balloff, if you hadn't done that I wouldn't have been able to send my kids to school, to buy them clothes to wear.' So we helped the community."

Another story comes from Roy Asbury, a Campbell County lawyer and one-time Tennessee state representative. It seems that on a frosty September morning in 1922, Asbury was a poor teenager who had to walk barefoot from his home in Caryville to Jacksboro High School. Balloff saw him on the road, called him into the store, and fitted the boy's feet with a good pair of shoes and socks. At the time, Asbury was so prejudiced against Jews that he left the store without even saying thank you. Yet that single incident changed his point of view, and the two men eventually were close friends, according to Asbury's son Lee, who became a circuit court judge. In 1962 Asbury the elder finally wrote a "thank you" to his friend Lou Balloff, saying the boy who was once prejudiced against all "furringers" had learned to "love and respect the Jews, and he developed a strong feeling of sympathy for all minority groups, oppressed groups, or individuals" and promised himself that someday he would do something to repay that kindness. Asbury apparently got his chance in 1944, when he served with the armed forces in Paris. That fall, he discovered an orphanage of three hundred children, nearly all Jewish, left in the care of an old Catholic priest and four nuns. One night the priest told him that sugar and sugar products were needed. Asbury and a friend obtained a truck, appropriated 1,500 pounds of sugar and 500 pounds of candy from the U.S. Army supply depot, and drove it to the orphanage before daylight. Before long, army personnel were furnishing food, clothing, medical supplies, and textbooks to the orphanage. The old priest and nuns tearfully approached Asbury's truck, trying to express their thanks in broken English. "The boy heard their expressions of thanks," Asbury wrote later, "but he knew they were not talking to him but to a man who, on a cold frosty morning, put a pair of shoes on the cold feet of a boy who was barefoot; and that boy knew he was trying to do something for the Jewish race to repay him for that pair of shoes, worn out more than 20 years before."

By the spring of 1929, the Balloffs' store in La Follette was doing well enough that Louis could spare investment cash to help Esther's brother Louis Sturm open a top-quality clothing store back in Middlesboro. Louis had begun several ventures in rural Appalachian towns, but nothing had quite worked out. This would change all that. Middlesboro was growing more affluent and could support a store with real class. It was scheduled for a grand opening that spring, offering high-end merchandise such as shoes for the extravagant price of ten and fifteen dollars a pair.

The Great Flood of 1929 intervened. Louis's son Mel, then a child of five, can still vividly remember being wakened in the late evening to go down to the store, which was safer ground because it had an upstairs office. He recalls looking out the upper-story window at a man clinging desperately to a light pole to escape the roiling waters and watching automobiles tumble end over end down the main street, which was like a rushing river. "Afterwards, the mud level in retail stores was six or seven feet deep," he says. "There was no insurance, and my father ended up owing the manufacturers for all that merchandise. By fall, the nation's whole economy was collapsing, too. My father wouldn't ever take bankruptcy, though. It took him years to get out of that hole."

After the flood, many Jewish merchant families left Middlesboro and Pineville. The Sturms moved to La Follette, where Louis Sturm went to work for Louis Balloff. Like all merchants, the Balloffs and Sturms suffered out the Depression, but they were clearly better off than most of their Appalachian neighbors. Using food provided by the new Federal relief agencies, Esther recruited several friends to help her cook enormous pots of soup and cereal, which they dragged down to the school to feed hungry children. "I had vats of cod liver oil full of vitamins, too, and I always forced them to have some of that if they wanted to get fed," she chortled. Esther believed that charity should come with a dose of education. "I remember when tramps would come to the door, I'd feed them and say, 'I'm a Jew, and I'm helping you. Always remember that, and if you say anything against Jews you're saying it against me.' I guess I always gave them a little lecture along with a handout!"

The two Balloff sons, Ed and Sam, helped out in the store before they were teenagers. Later on, their parents sent them to a private high school in Chattanooga, where they could have more contact with other Jewish families. The Balloffs went to synagogue on the High Holidays, first in Middlesboro and later in Knoxville. They taught their children basic prayers and kept Jewish observances as well as they could, though the pace of retail life could make things hectic. On Friday night, Esther lit her Shabbat candles in the store on the back of the stove they used for heat. Saturday, of course, was the busiest shopping day of the week. Passover, which called for a big family gathering, always seemed rushed because it coincided with Easter, when any who could afford it bought new clothes. Still, Esther always found time to take the train to Knoxville to buy kosher holiday foods at Ben Goodstein's grocery. In those pre-interstate days, the trip from La Follette took many hours, and automobiles frequently got stuck in Tennessee's clay mud. Mel recalls missing a much-anticipated childhood trip to the circus in Knoxville because roads were impassable. In his stairwell, he still has a framed picture of another early journey, in which the Sturm family car is mired in muck to the top of its oversize tires.

In 1949 Louis Sturm once again opened his own business, this time in nearby Jellico. Just a few months later, while escorting some high school students to an opera recital in Knoxville, he was killed in an automobile accident. Mel, then working in Chicago as a mechanical engineer, came home to tie up his father's business affairs. He stayed on to run the store, and later was elected the town of Jellico's youngest mayor at age twenty-nine.

Louis Sturm was buried in the Middlesboro, Kentucky, cemetery owned by the small Harlan County congregation. That synagogue had dwindled due to the Great Flood, worn out coal mines, and the end of railroad construction. When the synagogue shut down, the memorial plaques for deceased individuals (usually kept in a synagogue's sanctuary) were moved to a locked case in the cemetery, which was opened to relatives once a year for the traditional visit between Rosh Hashanah and Yom Kippur. After the case was vandalized, Mel Sturm went with his friends Bernie Shorr and Harry Marx to remove the plaques and install them permanently in the back wall of Heska Amuna Synagogue in Knoxville. Every year during times of general memorial, the light beside each name is faithfully turned on. Having none to remember them, we simply graft their memory on to our own. This is part of that basic imprint, I guess. Nobody is expendable. ∞

Five

*B*usiness *and* *P*olitics

oon on a weekday, October 1999. I'm strolling down a sidewalk on South Gay Street, heart and soul of Knoxville business for a century after the Civil War. Fifty years ago, Jewish businesses lined both sides of this major downtown avenue. Now only two are left, and one of those is moving out next year. Suburban flight choked the life out of this place in the 1970s, and quite frankly, it still looks comatose to the casual eye. Even on a lovely fall day at the height of lunch hour, the foot traffic is thin. Cars roll sluggishly over the broken pavement, and empty stores appear on every block. Yet closer examination shows new signs that South Gay Street might yet catch the national wave of downtown revitalization. A fragile crop of design-conscious offices and boutiques have begun to sprout at street level, while even grander transformations are hidden away on upper floors. Last weekend an organization called City People staged a walking tour of downtown apartments. During the past decade, about two hundred adventurous types have moved back into the urban grid, where tens of thousands once lived. These newest pioneers are professional people who obviously have enough money to renovate with artistry and glamour. The neighborhood doesn't have so much as a grocery or a drugstore, but the rooftop gardens look great, and I'm told the parties around here are really fabulous.

A featured stop on the City People tour, publicized with a lavish spread in our local newspaper, was the red brick Friedman

Building near the corner of Summit Hill and South Gay Street. A local attorney keeps her spacious, ultra-contemporary law office on the top floor, connected by a stairway to the second-story suite, where she lives with her husband, editor of the University of Tennessee's public policy journal. The arched doorways and large picture windows of the building provide a marvelous and unexpected backdrop to their collection of country antiques. Still, I'm kind of sorry they took down the sleek, 1940s wraparound sign for "Max Friedman, Jeweler" that hung across the front of the store for decades after it was vacated.

Max Friedman's grand old building used to dominate the busy corner of South Gay Street and Vine, heart of Knoxville's Jewish business district. Not long after his death in 1967, urban renewal created multilane Summit Hill Drive as an access road to Interstate 40 and the huge new Civic Coliseum complex. Crooked old Vine Street was completely replaced, except for a tiny, narrow lane that now branches off Summit Hill. Downtown business began its slow decline as the center of population shifted to west Knoxville and its new shopping centers.

About twenty years later, the first signs of urban resurrection appeared among the brick warehouses of the Old City, which includes a few square blocks on either side of Gay Street. Numbered among the success stories here is the upscale cabinetry and furnishings workshop of Ernie Gross, housed in the funky environs of an Old City warehouse at 515 Jackson Avenue. Of course, Ernie and his wife, psychologist Dr. Pam Gross, live in a suburban neighborhood out west, as do nearly all the Jews of Knoxville.

Up the street from Ernie Gross Designs, I can see half a dozen men gathered outside the Volunteer Ministry's day room at the corner of South Gay and Jackson. They smoke, talk quietly among themselves, and sift through worn packs of personal belongings. A few doors down from the shelter stands a hip, dilapidated thrift shop called Flashback, rubbing shoulders on the 100 block of South Gay with an attorney's office, an upscale furnishings store that looks like it may not last long, an experimental theater, and some kind of software company that hasn't quite unpacked its boxes yet. At 129 stands Martin and Lawrence Abrams's Mill Agent Store, where discount textiles are sold. The shop is pretty full this time of day, since even the west Knoxville soccer moms will trek all the way downtown for bargain prices on draperies and upholstery fabric. Still, the Abrams recently decided to relocate their store on the west end of town, where most of their customers live and shop.

The rest of the noontime foot traffic is heading next door to the other surviving Jewish business on this block, Harold's Kosher-Style Food Center. Across the laminate diner tables of this narrow little restaurant, the Abrams's cousin Harold Shersky and Harold's wife, Addie, have dished out a copious menu of Jewish deli for more than fifty years. I pop inside the door, greet Harold at the cash register, and buy a wedge of my favorite marble halvah, the crumbly sesame candy that shows up in every Jewish deli from Brooklyn to Banff. Maybe it's that mega-boost of sugar, calories, and cholesterol that melts away the drab veneer of 1999 reality. Suddenly, I can almost walk right into those days when America was flexing its postwar muscles, Harold and Addie were just starting out, and everybody in Knoxville agreed that Gay Street was the place to be.

Noon on a weekday, October 1949. As the clock strikes twelve, between sixty and seventy-five Jewish heads of households begin to emerge from their shops in an area that stretches roughly from Green's Hardware at 321 Northwest Gay Street (run by Sarah Robinson's brothers Ike and Jake) to Walter Blaufeld's cigar store at 616 South. Most of the Jewish business people cluster in a dense mass around the 100 and 200 blocks of South Gay Street on either side of Vine. They're coming out to eat lunch, deposit funds at the bank, check on the daily stock prices, or maybe stop in the street for a midday schmooze. Out of the many pawnshops along Gay and Vine Streets come Milton Gourse of Uncle Sam's Loan, Isadore Brody of American Loan, and various members of the big Slovis family. There's Diftler coming out of his Credit Jeweler's Shop at 200. I see the two Busch brothers, Harry and George, walking out from one of their several jewelry and loan companies in the 200 block of Gay. Business is pretty good. They are becoming rich men, and the crowds of shoppers in this fashionable part of downtown are so thick at times, you have to get off the sidewalk and weave your way through the automobile traffic. Gas rationing is a memory, and autos are everywhere. Two years ago, the last streetcar ran down Gay Street, carrying a Knoxville High School band that played "The Old Gray Mare." Luckily, the streetcars still run east up Magnolia Avenue and north to the Fourth and Gill area, two neighborhoods where most of the Jewish community now lives. These days, a housewife who wants kosher meat can phone in her order to the butcher, who hands the wrapped package to a streetcar conductor. The housewife collects it at the other end, paying the conductor a nickel for the meat's fare.

At five past noon I see Louis Joffe walking up the block from his SLOC ("Spend Less on Clothing") Shop down on Central. It's doubtful his customers are aware the shop's name is a pun on the word *schlock*, which is Yiddish for junk. That part of the Old City has a cheaper trade, catering mostly to the poor and out-of-town farmers. A. J. and Sylvia Robinson now sell used plumbing supplies from a storefront around the corner near Jackson and Central. They sold their Gay Street deli and switched to this business in the late 1930s, when TVA's rural electrification projects encouraged farmers to buy sinks and bathtubs for the first time. The flow of military and TVA construction surplus is still pretty good—but A. J.'s son Mitchell is a lot more intrigued by the rising tide of new home construction. With a small grubstake, he recently launched a business he calls Modern Supply, which aims to deal wholesale in upscale plumbing supplies for builders. Change is in the wind, and Jewish businessmen of the war-time generation are trying to catch its direction. A. J.'s brothers S. H. and Max are still in the junk business over on Cooper Street, while Glazer Steel at 2100 Ailor has begun to emerge as a powerhouse in the postwar scrap metal business.

Ten minutes after noon I finally spy the genial smile of Max Friedman, who comes out of his shop already deep in conversation with a city council crony. He was elected to council for his first two-year term in 1948. Behind him is C. B. ("Buster") Brown, whose Tennessee School of Beauty is housed in an upstairs suite adjoining Max Friedman's building. Not far away is Friedman's son-in-law Herbert Smullian, owner of Duchess Beauty Supply. Brown and Smullian dominate the fast-growing "beauty" business in Knoxville. Buster's school has actually been open since 1930, after his Austrian immigrant mother, Jean, went to a New York salon and paid twenty-five dollars a curl to

Max Friedman's jewelry store dominated the corner of Vine and Gay
Streets, flanked on either side by several dozen Jewish businesses. This
large crowd is gathered for the opening of his newly remodeled store,
circa 1949. Architect David Liberman, one of numerous Jewish
professionals who arrived during wartime, designed the work.
Courtesy of Scott Hahn.

learn the new machine method for making permanent waves. She
brought back the latest equipment, and the school managed to keep
afloat through the long Depression. Now the whole beauty industry
is poised for a takeoff, fueled by American women's eagerness to buy
products they couldn't get during the war.

In fact, the market for luxury goods has never been better.
Jewish businesses run by the immigrant generation—pawn shops, used
goods, and small groceries—are slowly being outnumbered by more
upscale concerns that deal in fine jewelry, shoes, and retail clothing.
Knoxville Jews noted the passing of an era when Morris Bart, the
former peddler who began his Clothing Emporium on Gay Street
before the turn of the century, died in 1943. Now half a dozen upscale, Jewish-owned dress shops appear on the fashionable end of Gay

Sterling House, 1949. Owned by the Levison family, it was the fanciest women's clothing shop in postwar Knoxville. Courtesy of Gilbert Levison and Natalie Robinson.

Street. One block west on Market Street, Morris Levison's Sterling House offers some of the classiest ladies' wear in town. He's so busy, he just brought in his niece Natalie in from Atlanta to work at the shop.

Isadore "Major" Millen has a shoe department at Sterling House, as well as a popular sandwich shop over on Gay and Jackson. He and his wife—both staunch members of Heska Amuna's Orthodox synagogue—hold an annual Easter egg hunt, which is quite popular with the area's Jewish children! Anyway, some of the downtown Jewish businessmen will grab a bite at Major's place or dine to the accompaniment of noontime organ music at the S&W Cafeteria. Others will stand at the bar for a plate of beans and knackwurst at Blaufeld's Cigar Store, near the grand old Tennessee Theater. Billig's Kosher Restaurant at 133 S. Gay is gone, after Louis Billig died a few years back. Now the Jewish merchants who want *hamische* fare drift over to Harold's new place at 131. Trade is busy enough to cover the main floor and downstairs, while in the upstairs compartment, Babe Fay's husband, Abe, operates billiard tables in his quiet "recreation center."

Knoxville merchant Isadore "Major" Millen, pictured here with his wife, Sara, and son, Stuart, hosted an annual Easter egg hunt, which was highly popular with local Jewish children in the 1940s. Courtesy of Knoxville Jewish Federation.

Harold Shersky, native Knoxville boy and cousin to the large Millen and Abrams clans, married his Louisville bride, Addie, in wartime and returned from service to manage one of the big chain shoe stores along Gay Street. In 1948 he took over the deli/restaurant, which had passed through various Jewish owners. Its most notorious proprietor was a certain Mr. Schieb, who sent shock waves through the Jewish community in the early 1940s when he was discovered selling "certified kosher" meat that he secretly bought at an ordinary Gentile meat-packing plant. Dr. Harold Winston, then a downtown optometrist, tells the story: "One morning, somebody saw Schieb go into the regular meat-packing place. He talked to a guy who worked there and got the whole truth. By noon it was all over the Jewish community. One by one, women started calling Schieb, saying 'Sorry, Mr. Schieb, I don't need my chicken today, we're dining out.' Old Schieb, he scratched his head over all these ladies suddenly deciding to dine out. Finally he figured it out." The story goes that a husky son of the

The large Millen family gathers at "Major's" vacation lodge in the 1940s. Courtesy of Harold Shersky.

Jewishly observant Glazer family publicly offered to go over and kill Schieb, who hastily got out of the kosher meat business.

All that's over now. Harold's father, Robert Shersky, runs the Kosher Meat Market near the Synagogue, though fewer of Knoxville's Jewish families keep completely kosher homes nowadays. Harold doesn't claim strict *kashrut* for his new restaurant, but he keeps a special meat cutter and dishes for those who want kosher fare, and Addie supplies kosher catering for Jewish events. Their restaurant is especially popular with corporate officers of the nearby Southern Railway Depot and executives at radio station WNOX across the street. Among the many country stars launched by WNOX is radio comedian Archie Campbell, who was hired for the station's popular "Midday Merry-Go-Round" after lasting only three hours in his first job as a waiter at Blaufeld's. (On the "Midday Merry-Go-Round," Knoxville Jews can also hear one of their own—Jewish country music fiddler Harry Nides, who was also a concertmaster for the Knoxville Symphony Orchestra.)

Harold's Deli is also crowded on Sunday mornings, when he serves free coffee to parents waiting for the kids to finish Sunday school at the Jewish Community Center on Vine and Broadway. Those are warm, sociable hours for young Jewish parents, though heated debates can erupt when Jewish Knoxvillians are comfortably among themselves. There was that day that somebody actually threw a chair, but mostly people get along, and they are conscious of the shared desire to show a quiet, respectable face to the Gentile community.

Often, the kids go back to the Center in the afternoon for sports and activities, part of the "Sunday Fun Day" program started this year. Social life revolves around the little Center building at Broadway and Vine, from the Yom Kippur break-the-fast dance in the fall to a grand Purim Ball in the spring. (The Yom Kippur dance is famous for getting couples together. It was here in 1942 that Sylvia Richer met Harold Leibowitz, a young man on temporary assignment as a TVA auditor with the Federal Government Accounting Office. They married in 1944 while Harold was in the Army Air Corps and settled here again after the war.)

The Center's bridge club sponsored a national tournament this year, and the amateur theater troupe puts on Yiddish plays in English. Temple Beth El, still located next door, held its eightieth anniversary gala at the Center in 1947, three years late because of the war. Mrs. Emily Strasburger (whose husband Charles manages a ladies' ready-to-wear shop on Market Street) wrote the script for an elaborate historical pageant, which involved dozens of Temple members dashing around in hoopskirts and Civil War uniforms. For this grand occasion, the Temple printed a glossy souvenir program bound in sapphire mock velvet and gold-embossed lettering. Ann Marcovitch's history of Knoxville Jews appears inside its pages, along with a listing of one hundred Temple families. Orthodox synagogue Heska Amuna, some blocks away on West Fifth Avenue and Broadway, has slightly more families—an oddity in the South, where Reform congregations tend to be larger. Over the years, the families of immigrant Eastern European stock, who tended to join the Orthodox Heska Amuna Synagogue, have multiplied their ranks at a greater rate than did the original German-Jewish merchants.

A 1948 census survey done by the Jewish Community Center showed 766 Jews in Knox County, out of 221,212 citizens listed in the

U.S. census for Knox County. Counting the merchants in outlying counties and the young community of Oak Ridge, the total number is probably still under 1,000. That same year, the whole community held a joyous all-day celebration of singing, dancing, and speechmaking to honor the new state of Israel. There's a local chapter of the Zionist District (headed by Prof. William Shaw), while Jake Corkland's wife, Mary, is a leader in regional Hadassah. Just this past summer, a pack of Knoxville kids went off to the Young Judaea convention and several attended the Zionist movement's summer camp.

Meanwhile, back on Gay Street, many wives and school-age children help out in their family businesses. Dora Green does the books in the hardware store run by her husband, Ike, and his brother Jake. They opened the store a few years ago in a building owned by their sister Sarah Green Robinson, who has accumulated some downtown real estate over the years. She's listed in the telephone directory as manager of Nathan's Auto Parts. Several women head their own clothing or jewelry shops along Gay Street, including the energetic Mrs. Sarah Tobe, who can stock the Fashion Shop at 201 by catching a predawn train to Atlanta and returning late the same day. One block west of Gay, Jewish shops are also clustered along Market Square, where Ben and Gus Deitch and Isadore Rosenblatt both operate small department stores. Harry Goldberger sells hardware and plumbing at Square Supply. Max Weinstein's shoe store is here, bordered by several Jewish-owned clothing shops. The Lippners still have their meat and fish stand in the big, smelly indoor environs of the Market House. One block down Market, I can follow my nose to the fresh, kosher pastries at Max and Ann Wolf's Quality Bakery at 510. The optometry office of Dr. Harold Winston used to be nearby at 502, but he recently moved into new offices down the block on the corner of Church Street.

Dr. Winston is still considered a new arrival, having moved to town with his wife Becky in 1942. A handful of Jewish professional men have appeared since the start of the war—some bringing their wives, others marrying local girls. Another big change is that many dozens of scientists and engineers from all over the country came to work on the top-secret Manhattan Project in the federal installation at Oak Ridge, an hour away. The secret government town of Oak

Ridge was built up from the Tennessee mud almost overnight behind barred security gates. The number of Jewish scientists declined at the end of wartime research on the atomic bomb, as Oak Ridge's population dropped from its wartime high of 75,000 to just over 30,000. However, more of these new young Ph.D.'s are on their way back as the Atomic Energy Commission proceeds with its plans to build a research center in Oak Ridge. The new AEC, headquartered in Washington, D.C., is led by yet another ethnically Jewish scientist, David Lilienthal, who lived in Knoxville during the 1930s as head of TVA. Lilienthal was back in Knoxville just last March, when the fences officially came down around the new, open civilian city in ceremonies attended by hosts of celebrities. The Jewish merchants on Gay Street are watching this new town for opportunities. The word is that Mrs. Glazer's enterprising son Guilford is planning to lease federal land for a new shopping center.

At any rate, the young, well-educated Jewish population of Oak Ridge has just officially chartered its own synagogue—a sign, perhaps, of a certain cultural divide between this new job-centered professional class and the old merchant families of Knoxville. Of course, Knoxville has men like University of Tennessee professors William Shaw, Simon Marcovitch, and Salo Engels, as well as Ben Winick and Max Morrison, who both keep their law offices in the downtown Hamilton Bank Building. A few blocks down the street is Joe Levitt Sr., respected city editor of the *Knoxville New-Sentinel*. Still, on this fall day in 1949, you could probably fit all the Jewish doctors, dentists, lawyers, engineers, architects, and college professors in Knoxville around a single lunch table. That's true in most American towns. Jews still tend to run stores and own businesses, though it looks to be a very different story for their sons and daughters. Prosperity, expanded opportunity, and the GI Bill have combined to send a record number of Jewish young people off to college these days. A couple of years ago, Rabbi Leo Stillpass at the Temple started a Hillel group for the small but vibrant Jewish crowd at the University of Tennessee.

Notes, October 1999. As the sugar high is wearing off, I fast-forward through time and stroll down to Market and Union. (This corner, anchored by the handsome old Arnstein Building, is ironically Knoxville's traditional "preaching corner," where generations of street fundamentalists are allowed to harangue passersby.) In 1951 Sam Morrison opened a nine-foot-wide record store called Bell Sales Company a short distance from where I'm standing at 22½ Market Square. Sam's father had come to Knoxville as a tailor in the 1920s. Sam married Virginia Joffe, who was the daughter of a Knoxville dry goods merchant and the cousin of Louis Joffe at the SLOC Shop, down in the Old City. Even in the 1950s, practically everybody was related. If a dance or bar mitzvah party was celebrated at the Center, Sam and Virginia Morrison were always there to spin the records. The last songs were always "Good Night, Irene," and "Good Night, Sweetheart."

At Bell Sales Company you could listen to a new recording for a dime, which came off the price if you bought it, and if you didn't buy, it was put into a collection for the March of Dimes. By 1954, rock 'n' roll was already competing with country music. Sam kept up with the trends, though he was more of a Mantovani and show tunes fan himself. A west Knoxville group called the Everly Brothers could be heard on local radio, but they weren't famous yet. That year, a Memphis teenager cut his first single at Sun Studios. Sam Morrison got several boxes of this shellac seventy-eight record, which he sometimes played over loudspeakers for the farmers stacking produce at the Market House. Brad McKuen, a traveling executive for RCA Records, used to stop in at Sam's store because he firmly believed that anything popular at Bell Sales in Knoxville was destined to go nationwide. That day in 1954, Sam told him the store was selling a box a day of this new single, an R & B tune that was, against all convention, being purchased by the white country and pop audiences as well as a black R & B audience. Brad McKuen bought two copies of "That's All Right, Mama," sent one to his superiors at RCA, and reported that young Elvis Presley had already sold five thousand records in Knoxville. A year later, Elvis signed with RCA and became an international sensation. Quiet Sam Morrison never made a big deal about this, and the story was little known until it showed up years later in the Elvis biography *Last Train to Memphis*. (Though Sam's older daughter is my friend Mary Linda Schwarzbart, the first time I heard the tale was in Jack Neely's "Secret History" column for *MetroPulse*.)

Twenty years after Elvis found stardom, almost all the Jewish businesses were gone from this area. Market Square held a discount department store, a cheap bar, a liquor dealer, and a few sandwich shops. The eastern side of Market Street's 500 block was leveled to create a bank parking lot. All through the late 1970s I gazed out over this desolate blacktop acreage from my window office on the fourth floor of the Arnstein Building, where I worked as an editor for 13-30 Corporation (later called Whittle Communications). About this time a philanthropic soul named Charlie Krutch left funds in his will for the parking lot to be turned into an urban green space. As luck would have it, one of the landscape designers was Peggy Leibowitz Hedrick (one of Harold and Sylvia's three children). Krutch Park is a lovely site in downtown Knoxville. Greek pillars and wrought-iron gates enclose a block-long oasis of tall, rustling trees and flower gardens. Near the spot where Dr. Winston's office and Quality Bakery once stood, sandwich eaters now lunch beneath an airy gazebo overlooking an arched wooden bridge across a small lily pond. Urban renewal has often been unkind to this historic neighborhood, so it's nice to know that occasionally the city fathers can unpave a parking lot and put up a paradise.

Some weeks earlier I sat in the west Knoxville condominium of Dr. Harold Winston, who helped me sketch a rough map of the downtown Jewish businesses. (I later double-checked his map with six other native and longtime Knoxville Jews and the 1949 city directory, but the initial sketch proved admirably accurate.) Dr. Winston, who was president of Temple Beth El and the Jewish Community Center when these institutions were first moving away from downtown, has made it his avocation to gather and document early Jewish events in the community. He wrote a history for Temple Beth El's centennial in 1964 and made a documentary film of the community's beginnings to mark the Temple's major renovation in the 1980s. From a bulging accordion file in his office, he was able to pull out a welter of miscellaneous goodies. There were photos of a 1911 Temple Beth El Sunday school picnic, old newspaper clippings, even a vintage 1867 shot of Gay Street before it was paved.

That day, he told me the story of Max Kesselman, a Jew who came down from Chicago in the late 1930s as the representative of a scrap iron concern. Kesselman was supposed to buy up the defunct Smoky Mountain Railroad stock for scrap, but the sharp-eyed executive noticed that TVA was planning to build Douglas Dam along this route and would need a means to haul materials. He borrowed a few thousand dollars to buy the railroad himself, then immediately leased it to TVA for the outrageous sum of $10,000 per month. This went on for a couple of years, after which the railroad was leased by rural Sevier County to use as local transport. By the time Kesselman scrapped his engines and sold off valuable depot land in downtown Knoxville, the initial investment of a few thousand dollars in the Southern Railroad and Equipment Company had grown into a substantial fortune. Gene Rosenberg of Heska Amuna tells me the people in small East Tennessee communities (where Jewish population has always been negligible) routinely use the phrase "a real East Tennessee Jew" to express grudging admiration for anybody (Jewish or not) with unusual business acumen. One has to wonder if they got the idea from Max Kesselman's "junk train."

Such comments about Jewish business sense were always a common thing in East Tennessee, where the expression "he jewed me down" (that is, bargained me down to a lower price) is even today inserted into conversation by people who don't give the slightest thought to its ethnic derivation. It shocked me the first time I heard it in the 1970s, a week after moving here from California. When I mentioned my distress to the speaker, he seemed quite mortified at having said something that could be construed as bigoted. Much has changed in the modern South.

At least in the postwar era, most native Jews seemed to take such expressions of Jewish business acumen with ironic good humor. As a tiny minority selling its goods in a sea of Baptists, they generally felt it was better not to rock the boat. Occasionally, an encounter brought out somebody's ornery streak. Joe Goodstein tells a story about his father, Ben, who ran the grocery on Luttrell Avenue. In 1950 it happened that a prominent and well-to-do member of the Temple, Mr. Sam Averbuch of the People's clothing store, had recently passed away. A regular customer of Ben Goodstein's, a Gentile named Mr.

Lemon, came into the store one day. Slyly, he asked, "Now, Mr. Goodstein, you Jews know everything about each other. You can tell me, one friend to another—just how much did Mr. Averbuch leave?" He kept pestering Ben on this subject until the grocer lost patience. He answered, "Mr. Lemon, if you keep it a secret just between us, I'll tell you exactly how much Mr. Averbuch left." The other man drew closer. Pulling himself up to the full extent of his diminutive height, Ben Goodstein then announced, "The truth, Mr. Lemon, is that Mr. Averbuch left *everything*. He didn't take anything with him!"

It's worth mentioning that the merchant Jews of Knoxville were in fact very interconnected with regard to finances and business dealings, as were the Jews of most small communities. One obvious reason was that kinship ties made it quite natural to approach each other for business start-up loans, partnerships, or entry-level jobs for one's children. Such ties were reinforced by the fact that Gentile bankers were not particularly eager to make business loans to Jews, and federal laws did not yet require them to overcome such reluctance. (In this respect, the eventual change in federal equal lending laws—making it easier for Jews and other ethnic groups to compete for banks loans—served to loosen the interdependence of Knoxville Jews in subsequent years.)

A third reason may have been that close social relationships among the town's Jews (in a time when most did not mix freely in the Gentile circles) encouraged the habit of including each other in new ventures. One good example, related to me by Dr. Winston, was the time another member of the community let him in on a deal to buy a large shipment of plastic rope. The goods were then shipped overseas, made into purses, and peddled to tourists in Gatlinburg at a tidy profit.

Just why the most affluent and respectable Jews in southern towns were excluded from Gentile social life is a complicated matter, rarely aired in public during this time. Social interaction could be quite free and open in smaller, more isolated towns such as La Follette (where the merchant Balloffs felt quite accepted) or Jellico (where bright young men such as Mel Sturm were quickly involved in civic affairs). Yet in larger communities with an established social hierarchy, a more restrictive pattern emerged. Southerners freely did business with Jews, in many cases elected them to city council or other public office, and maintained a reasonable albeit distant tolerance for their Old Testament beliefs. All other interactions were governed by the famous "Five O'Clock Shadow," a kind of tacit apartheid that excluded Jews (as well as blacks and several other ethnic groups) from social events outside business hours, such as parties and gatherings at clubs and fraternal organizations. Due to a variety of political and social shifts, this pattern of social exclusion and popular anti-Semitism was already disappearing with amazing speed in most of the United States by the late 1940s, according to historian Leonard Dinnerstein. However, in more socially established towns of the South, such attitudes would remain in force for at least two more decades. Mark Bauman (editor of *Southern Jewish History*) tells me that as late as the 1970s, a millionaire Atlanta Jewish businessman he interviewed still referred bitterly to that "Five O'Clock Shadow" that made Jews as unacceptable at social events as a day's-end bristle of beard.

Although Jews didn't move in Knoxville's loftier social scenes during the 1940s and 1950s, some had notable impact in government. Ben and Frank Winick were heavily involved in the political scene during the Depression and wartime eras, while their brother-in-law Charles Siegel was a longtime city councilman and vice mayor from 1944 to 1945. Later on, Max Wolf of Quality Bakery (a.k.a. Harold Shersky's brother-in-law) held a Knox County commissioner's slot for decades. Myra Corkland Weinstein's aunt, Amelia Strauss, was a juvenile court judge. However, the most political Jew in Knoxville from the early 1930s onward was jeweler Max Friedman. With his perky bow tie, wide smile, and sharp eyes behind wire-rimmed glasses, later photos of this Eastern European immigrant show a strong resemblance to Harry Truman. The jeweler, who never lost his heavy accent, was said to admire this up-by-his-bootstraps merchant who became president. According to Joe Billig (who worked in his uncle's store during the 1940s before switching to Duchess Beauty Supply), Max Friedman was one of very few businessmen in Republican Knoxville who not only supported Truman against Dewey in 1948 but also bet a large sum of money on him in the downtown

Charles Siegel *(second row, far right)*, brother-in-law of Ben Winick,
served on the city council through much of the 1930s and was vice
mayor in 1944. Courtesy of Knoxville Jewish Federation.

election pools. (Since the Civil War, when East Tennessee sided with
the Union, Republicans have been more numerous than Democrats
in this area, particularly among the business classes. However, local
Democrats have often become prominent on the city council and
state party level.)

It was through his work as a state committeeman for the Democratic Party that Max Friedman reportedly made an enduring mark
on national history. The story was told by his close friend Robert
("Uncle Bob") Smith that Max and he visited Franklin Roosevelt at
the Albany governor's mansion in August of 1932, just before FDR's
ascent to the presidency. In their presence, the candidate opened a
wire from party leader Jim Farley, who urged the immediate adoption
of a strong campaign slogan. "FDR declared we would hold an election then and there," recounted Smith. "He asked us for suggestions.
I came up with 'Shareholders of America.' FDR nodded, but Max said
he would have to disagree. He announced that what the American
people wanted was a New Deal." The next day, medallions were struck

« Let's Finish the Job **Right !** »

VOTE FOR

MAX FRIEDMAN

... FOR ...

COUNCILMAN

City-at-Large
From SIXTH DISTRICT

Your Support Will Be Appreciated
—See Other Side

Max Friedman was a popular city councilman from 1948 until his sudden death in 1968. As a state Democratic Party official in the 1930s, he was said to have suggested the phrase "New Deal" to Franklin Roosevelt. Courtesy of Scott Hahn.

with the phrase that would carry FDR to the White House. (This anecdote later appeared in Max Friedman's obituary in the *New York Times*.)

In addition to many leadership positions within the Jewish community, Max Friedman served nearly two decades on the city council, as well as terms on the county court, county election commission, and Knoxville Housing Authority. When reasoning with an opponent, he often began with a disarming smile, followed by the phrase, "I'll be frank with you." He was also known for lightening the mood of tense debates with his own wit. One time, just after he arm wrestled a local real estate company into saving the city $60,000 in condemnation costs on a planned public project, he leaned across to a reporter and whispered, "That's what I call Jewishprudence."

During the latter days of his political career, Friedman ran for reelection to council during a heated debate over a referendum to repeal the local ban on liquor sales. Candidate Friedman was cornered at a civic club luncheon by a group of prohibitionist ministers who demanded to know his views. "I'll be frank with you," he told them. "I think it's a greater sin to tell a lie than to take a drink. And I'm not going to tell you a lie. I am going to vote for legal liquor." About two miles east of the Synagogue and Temple buildings on

A 1940 Passover seder with the large Friedman-Billig-Smullian clan, plus a few friends. Courtesy of McClung Historical Collection.

Kingston Pike, you can find a bronze plaque to Max Friedman on the Cumberland Avenue overpass named in his honor. Fittingly, this overpass connects downtown with a highway to the airport. As councilman, Max Friedman reportedly insisted upon paving the dirt runways of Knoxville's new airfield, because he predicted the town would someday attract jet airplane traffic.

We can't leave Max Friedman's story without adding this final detail: In 1951 he arranged for his cousin Israel Gruenberg, Israel's married daughter Frieda Schwarzbart, her husband, Isadore, and nine-year-old son, Arnold, to be brought out of Vienna, Austria, in the aftermath of World War II. He also brought Frieda's two brothers—Paul Gruenberg, who settled in New York, and Dr. Julius Gruenberg, who settled in Knoxville with his wife, Mary, and son, Joe. In order to accomplish this task, Arnold Schwarzbart tells me, Max Friedman had to post a quarter-million-dollar cash bond from his own funds and push a special bill through Congress. You might say this action closed a circle. In 1912 Israel Gruenberg bought a ticket to America for teen-age immigrant Max Friedman.

In the next generation, Adrian Burnett and David Blumberg followed Max Friedman into political prominence. Adrian Burnett's father, Max, came to Knoxville from Poland at the turn of the century and bought a dairy farm north of town in the area now called Halls. Adrian acquired more land for beef and milk production and eventually got involved in Halls politics through the school board. He served on the county school board for many years, and after his death in 1972 a new school building was named Adrian Burnett Elementary in his honor.

David Blumberg was actually born in tiny Cotton Plant, Arkansas, where his was the only Jewish family. (The story was told in his family that Jerome Mark, beloved 1920s rabbi at Temple Beth El, got on a handcar in Knoxville and pumped all the way to Cotton Plant to circumcise David Blumberg's younger brother. This may be an exaggeration, but it suggests that Knoxville rabbis ministered to a wide area during this period.) The Blumbergs weren't a Jewishly observant family, but David somehow got involved in B'nai B'rith's AZA fraternity for Jewish high school boys in the region. Late in 1929, he came to Knoxville on a combined academic and football scholarship to the University of Tennessee. The money ran out two years later, and he had to finish his degree at Washington University in St. Louis. However, during his early Knoxville tenure, young Dave Blumberg spent most of his free time playing ball in the new Jewish Community Center and making connections with local Jewish merchants. He sought advice from the wealthy Max Arnstein, went to services at the Temple, and joined the local B'nai B'rith men's lodge. On weekends between football games he earned extra dollars working at Jacob Reich's store on Vine Street. That's where he met Jacob's daughter Miriam, who would become his first wife after he returned to Knoxville in 1936.

At first Blumberg worked in a plumbing store, then got a job as a weekend broadcaster for WNOX. After his war service, he opened up a successful life insurance office on Gay Street. The business was going strong by the 1950s, so the energetic David Blumberg sought new fields to conquer. Throughout the decade, he held a variety of civic positions in organizations such as the Chamber of Commerce, United Way, and the Library Board. At one point he had to face down the White Citizens Council when they wanted to use the library auditorium for a large rally. He finally got elected to city council in 1966, the year after Max Friedman died. Unlike Friedman, Blumberg didn't relish local politics, particularly since he shared that era's council table with the famously opinionated grocer Cas Walker, a Knoxville institution for many decades. After five years on the council, Blumberg turned his attention to the international Jewish scene. He had stayed involved in B'nai B'rith, gradually working his way up in the local, district, and national organizations to head the B'nai B'rith Youth Commission from 1959 to 1965. In 1971 he was elected international president of B'nai B'rith. Though he was the first unopposed candidate since 1925, many Knoxville Jews traveled up to the Philadelphia convention just to cast their vote for a local boy made good. During the next seven years, which saw a huge growth in B'nai B'rith's youth enrollment, David Blumberg traveled the world meeting presidents and kings, attending White House dinners, and even weekending at Camp David. In later years, Blumberg treasured a group photo of presidents Carter, Begin, and Sadat, autographed by all three men to "our good friend David." Not long after this, David and Miriam Blumberg were divorced, and David moved to Washington, D.C., after marrying the widow of an Atlanta rabbi prominent in the civil rights movement.

During the 1940s, a small wave of newcomers began to settle here with ideas that subtly changed the texture of Knoxville Jewish life. A handful of men who would figure prominently among the next generation's Jewish leadership came to town on federal or wartime projects. Optometrist Dr. Harold Winston and architect David Liberman, who moved here with their wives, became part of this new infusion. A handful of others—such as the aforementioned Harold Leibowitz—joined the existing cousins club by marrying local girls. Among this group was Homer Kramer, who arrived as a government accountant and stayed to marry William Shaw's daughter Genevieve. (Homer's twin sister, Helen, came down for the wedding festivities and ended up marrying Joe Billig.) Before long, Yankee professional men such as Harold Leibowitz and Ted Reback (who married Dolly Robinson) began to show up as officers of the Temple, Synagogue, and the Jewish Community Center. Not all the newcomer-leaders were men. Another arrival was Sylvia Silver, who moved to Knoxville in 1940 with her musician husband, Leo, two-year-old daughter, Jane ("and a yellow canary," she informs me with her trademark precision). Sylvia immediately became caught up in the Temple, the Center, and the local Hadassah chapter. Worrying about her Jewish neighbors who needed rides to the doctor or help with family crises eventually led to her longtime position as chair of the Social Services Committee for the Knoxville Jewish Federation. As such, she joined a notable line of women who pioneered social services in Southern Jewish communities.

By far the largest group of professional men in this era flowed into Oak Ridge, which eventually attained the status of having the largest number of Ph.D.'s per capita of any town in the nation. During the war years, a sizable community of Jewish engineers and scientists appeared almost overnight to work on the super-secret Manhattan Project in Oak Ridge. (David Liberman also came to Oak Ridge during this time to work as an architect during the town's phenomenal building boom.) By 1944 the Jewish Oak Ridgers had organized their own regular services and by the following year had begun a Sunday school with six children. The start of this story is best told in the words of the late Oak Ridge journalist Ruth Carey. A cousin to Joe Goodstein, Carey was raised in Knoxville. As a young married woman shopping in downtown Knoxville in the early 1940s, she remembers overhearing the grumbled comments of Knoxville citizens about "*those* people—people from New York and all kinds of places. Aliens." Soon Ruth's husband, Milton, got a job in Oak Ridge and commuted daily on the "stretch-out," a long vehicle that appeared to be two cars welded together. What is now a journey of perhaps forty minutes took about two hours over bumpy, dusty, or mud-dry roads. In mid-1944, the Careys finally obtained housing in Oak Ridge. "A few days after the move, I went to Knoxville by bus. It was impossible to wipe mud from my shoes. I walked into a store and people looked at me forbiddingly. I knew I was perceived as an Oak Ridger. I had become an alien in my own hometown."

It would be hard to minimize how oddly the locals must have regarded this brand-new, culturally different town that arose so quickly on southern soil with such a strong northeastern-Jewish character in its beginnings. Writing in celebration of the Oak Ridge Jewish Congregation's fortieth anniversary in 1984, Ruth Carey continues the tale:

> Oak Ridge was the Secret City of World War II— a fenced-in, tightly guarded military reservation. It swarmed with people working around the clock. The plants and the city arose "overnight" to contain 80,000 military and civilian workers and family members. The military personnel—GIs with scientific and technical capabilities—were plucked out of Army units to find themselves in an odd, not-on-the-map place called Oak Ridge. Many were Jewish.
>
> The Army made the Chapel on the Hill available for worship by people of all faiths. With services on Friday nights, Jews had an advantage over Protestant and Catholic groups, who had to wait their turn hour by hour on Sundays. However, we were always pleased to stand aside for young love if one of the frequent weddings was taking place. As soon as the newlyweds exited amid a sprinkle of rice (wartime rationing was in effect) we'd go inside and our services would begin, conducted in turn by a parade of men from everywhere—many in uniform. The early services were coordinated by Major William Bernstein—founder of our Congregation. He was a physician serving in the Army and became head of the hospital.

In 1943, Dr. Bernstein came down from the University of Minnesota to organize medical services in the new installation. "There was no housing in Oak Ridge in July '43, only dorms," he related in an audiotape made a few years before his death in the late 1980s.

We found a lot of mud, inadequate facilities for food, clothing, and other necessities, and a strange mixture of people. Shortly after the High Holy Days, the "Mayor of Oak Ridge," Captain O'Mear, told Mr. Cohen [operator of a local laundry] that the newly built Chapel-on-the-Hill was available, and if there was a Jewish group, time would be set aside. Cohen asked me to look into this, and we gathered informally for the first time in fall of 1943. On Passover, April 1944, we invited people to our homes but found there were still many who had no place to go for a seder.

Given the large number of unconnected Jews showing up in the area, the little group decided to hold a community seder during the next two years. Bernstein's wife, Mildred, Ruth Carey, and several other Jewish women made matzah ball soup for 250.

"It was amazing to discover there were so many Jews in Oak Ridge, though so few attended our services," Bernstein observed later. (One notable Jewish scientist in Oak Ridge was nuclear pioneer Alvin Weinberg, who directed the Oak Ridge Laboratory for eighteen years, though he never affiliated with the Oak Ridge Jewish community.) As happens today, Jews seemed to appear out of the woodwork during the High Holidays. In fall of 1944 the Jewish Welfare Board in New York sent down a visiting rabbi with prayer books and a shofar—after solemnly promising the government not to question the rabbi afterward about how many Jews had turned up for services—or anything else he saw in the Secret City.

"Here was a town literally being built around us," recalls Mildred Landay, who arrived with her husband Nathan in 1944. "Everything happened with amazing speed. A field became a street in a day's time. Boardwalks materialized to cover the ever-present mud. This raw, unfinished town was a study in contrasts. The secret, fenced city had three grocery stores to serve 75,000 people. Meat, which was rationed, was almost impossible to get and was likely to be spoiled; food poisoning was too common to mention. Shopping was a real test of endurance and patience. Once in a while, we made a trip to Knoxville in an Army trailer bus, the symbolic covered wagon for Oak Ridge pioneers. . . . We came here newly married and this was our first home," she adds. "We, like almost everyone else, had no family to depend on, and friends quickly became extended family."

That same year, a Ladies Auxiliary (later Sisterhood) was organized, even though the congregation wouldn't be officially chartered until 1949. During the first several years, every Ladies Auxiliary president was pregnant, a sure sign the community was young and growing. "We had no history," comments Herb Hoffman, who was twenty-seven when he and his wife, Myra, moved to Oak Ridge in December of 1944. "The congregation was begun by people who were mostly my age, and very few had any organizational connection with synagogues at the time. We got involved because it was a young congregation just starting. We had to work it out as we went along, and people were open to new ways of doing things." Hoffman was sent to Los Alamos Laboratory in New Mexico a year later, but he and his wife returned in 1950 and have remained in Oak Ridge ever since. "I was president three different times," adds Hoffman. "That would never have happened if I stayed in Baltimore." Myra Hoffman, a trained educator, also headed the religious school during this time.

After the war, Oak Ridge saw an influx of nuclear scientists and engineers, including many new young Jewish Ph.D.'s. When the security fences came down in 1949, the Jewish Congregation of Oak Ridge was one of the first religious organizations to obtain a plot for its new structure. "The Building," as it was known, was literally constructed by its young members, who personally dug the foundation and built it up, block by block, on nights and weekends. It was a square, basic building made of concrete blocks, designed for them pro bono by Knoxville Jewish architect Sam Good. "An unforgettable sight was a whole minyan of men raising the huge, heavy beams that support the roof, evoking visions of the ancient Jews building the Pyramids," wrote Ruth Carey later. "But this time they were their own volunteer slaves and masters. The women helped, too—some digging and hammering—and all brought food in a steady stream to the hardworking laborers." This basic building—gradually expanded over the decades— was dedicated in 1952, and two years later the congregation had grown large enough to hire its first rabbi, Martin Kessler.

On a bitterly cold day in January 1955, industrialist Guilford Glazer broke ground for a new shopping center on leased federal land in the government enclave of Oak Ridge, Tennessee. The shopping center's architect, David Liberman, is pictured in the second row, fourth from the end; in the front row are Mel and Fran Sturm, who would own Sturm's Youth World, sitting next to Homer Kramer, who owned Kramer Shoes. Courtesy of Mel and Fran Sturm.

The growth of Oak Ridge as a civilian town opened opportunities for new businesses. Samuel's, a men's clothing store run by Sam Miller, had been operated on the reservation since 1942. Sam was instrumental in starting up the Oak Ridge Congregation, but in 1952 he left the store in the hands of a nephew and bought an upscale Gay Street men's clothing shop called Shriver's, which he ran for the next two decades. About this time, Homer Kramer was looking to lease space from the government for a new store. He and his new wife, Genevieve, were good friends with Mel Sturm out in Jellico. He agreed to invest in Homer's new shoe store as a way of testing the business waters in this new town. As Kramer-Sturm Shoes (later Kramer Shoes) began to flourish, the enterprising Guilford Glazer (son of Oscar Glazer, whose story appears in the last chapter) was thinking big. You still couldn't own private acreage in the new town, but he approached the government about developing a town shopping center on leased

Mel Sturm, who was elected Jellico, Tennessee, mayor at age
twenty-nine, mugs with Santa in front of his store, 1954.
Courtesy of Mel and Fran Sturm.

land. About that time, Mel Sturm and his new bride, Frances Alper of
Chattanooga, had decided tiny Jellico was not the right place to raise
a Jewish family. They liked Oak Ridge because this unique small town
of fewer than 30,000 was almost entirely populated by young, middle-
income people with a high educational level. Best of all, the growing
Jewish community now contained more than seventy families, including nearly the same number of children. In fact, the whole town was
booming with babies (it had one of the highest birthrates in the nation
at that time) so Guilford Glazer asked him to bring a children's store
into the new Oak Ridge Shopping Center. Mel and his brother Evan
opened Sturm's Youth World, later expanding to a second store in
Knoxville. Max Friedman and Harold Shersky both operated stores
in Oak Ridge for a time.

"A businessman in Oak Ridge was rather unique back then,
because almost everyone in town was employed in science," Mel says.

"When Guilford was finishing the shopping center, I sent Fran down to apply for housing. There was no private ownership of homes, you see. Fran came back almost in tears because they said, 'Sorry, lady, there's no housing for merchants here, you have to be a scientist.' So I told her to go back and beg, which she did, and they finally gave us a two-bedroom garden apartment." Oak Ridgers wouldn't start owning their own houses until a decade after the war's end.

Back in Knoxville, the war and its aftermath produced one of the community's enduring institutions, a newsletter called the *Center Menorah*. It began when Jewish Community Center director Milton Collins wanted to keep in touch with the one hundred Knoxville Jewish boys in wartime service. Collins also kept a personal correspondence with many of these young men, who had grown up playing ball and attending dances at the Center. His letters are gone, but Barbara Bernstein keeps a shoebox with the soldiers' replies—full of blackouts by the censors, references to battles, and the cheerful determination to sound upbeat about the whole thing. One of these boys was Harold Leibowitz, the young accountant who had met his wife Sylvia at the Yom Kippur dance in the Center on Vine Street. He had enlisted in the Army Air Corps, was captured, and spent part of the war in a prison camp, where he sent and received letters from Milton Collins.

Like the *Center Menorah* he created and edited from 1943 until his retirement in 1963, Collins was intimately involved in the flow of community events. He was born on Vine Street, where his mother, Pearl, once hosted the little basement *cheder*. He and his brother Abe played on the Center basketball team, where Milton acquired the nickname "Dead-Eye" for his shooting prowess. Both brothers were stricken with muscular dystrophy as young men. Abe, a talented violinist for the Knoxville Symphony, was eventually bedridden. Milton worked as long as he could as a bookkeeper for United Loan. He was already managing the Center on an informal basis by 1942, when the community appointed the now crippled young man as its first Center director. A year later, he started the monthly *Center Menorah*, in which the gossip column "Suzy Snoops" examined everything from upcoming *simchas* to reports on who was seen ogling whom at a recent high school mixer.

Milton Collins, beloved director of the Jewish Community Center from 1942 to 1963. Courtesy of Knoxville Jewish Federation.

For the next two decades, as the postwar baby boomers passed through the Center's nursery school, Sunday school, and summer day camps, Milton Collins was the one to whom Jewish children brought joys and troubles. The temporary appointment became a permanent, much-more-than-full-time job. "Milton Collins was the most wonderful man. He raised our generation," says Myra Weinstein. "If any of us had a problem, we went to him for help and he told us what to do. The guys in particular loved him so much. When he got so ill he couldn't walk, they would pick him up and carry him into the movies." Adds Arnold Schwarzbart, "If any Jewish child in Knoxville ever wanted anything—a basketball, a Band-Aid, a book—it was most likely to be located on the second shelf of the cabinet in Milton Collins's office. In all the years I knew him, I never once saw him lose his temper."

Speaking of Arnold Schwarzbart, I was tickled to find a back issue of the *Center Menorah*, which includes a photo of Sunday school students attending a model Passover seder. Arnold, who had emigrated from Europe just four years before, sits in the foreground of this photo, next to Sam Morrison's daughter, Mary Linda. His arm rests casually on the back of her chair, and she leans forward as if pretending not to notice. He's thirteen, she's eleven, and they both look extremely serious. Well they should, for later they would claim this seder as their first date. Arnold and Mary Linda were an item all the way from preadolescence through college, marrying right after graduation from the University of Tennessee when Mary Linda was still young enough to need her father's signed permission to get a marriage license. (The early conditioning stuck, for as adults they would continue to devote much time to Jewish communal service. Arnold would later be president of the Synagogue, the Jewish Community Center, the Knoxville Jewish Federation, and various other local Jewish organizations; Mary Linda would be president of Hadassah and the Knoxville Jewish Federation.)

The *Center Menorah*'s ninth and tenth anniversary issues, printed in 1951 and 1952, provide an intriguing glimpse into postwar Jewish life in Knoxville. Its pages show the World War II generation firmly in charge, including many of the professional men and women who came during wartime. We see architect David Liberman reelected to another term as Center president (to be succeeded by Harold Winston a year later). An article reports on the 1951 study of Knoxville Jewish population from a survey committee headed by Sylvia Silver. Interestingly, the survey showed that Knoxville's Jewish population rose slightly from 1948—from 766 to 796 persons—but lost 27 families. The largest increase in members occurred in the age six to fourteen bracket. The survey notes that Knoxville has one of the smallest Jewish communities per capita among cities with a population of 150,000 to 250,000. Growth in the Knoxville Jewish community failed to keep pace with growth in Knox County, which gained nearly 1,500 people during the same period. This loss of Jewish numbers relative to total population growth was occurring all over the South as a result of declining business opportunities and the out-migration of younger college graduates. This decline would only be halted several decades hence in those southern communities where industry, universities, and research centers brought in new populations of Jewish professionals.

In light of these still tiny numbers, it's amazing to turn a few pages in the 1951 issues and read that six leaders from Knoxville are in the "top brass" of national Jewish organizations. "Regional presidents of the ZOA [Zionist Organization of America] and Hadassah are Ben Winick and Mrs. J. B. Corkland. Stanley (Spud) Robinson [Sarah Robinson's son] has been elected to lead the Southern Region of the Intercollegiate Zionist Federation of America. David Blumberg and Mrs. Harry (Amelia) Strauss are serving B'nai B'rith as presidents of the men's and women's groups of District Seven and the National Vice President of the Federation of Temple Sisterhoods is Mrs. C.C. (Emily) Strasburger." ("It was such a small town back then," Barbara Bernstein explained to me later. "If you were smart, you had to look outside of Knoxville to realize your talents.") In any case, three of the Knoxville leaders in that article would serve on the national boards of those Jewish organizations within a decade.

In the pages of the *Center Menorah* old family names still outnumber the new. Nathan Robinson wins a 1951 Chevrolet in the annual Center raffle but donates back $250. Mitchell Robinson writes the sports column and serves on the board. We see a glamorous photo of Sarah Robinson, then president of Heska Amuna Sisterhood. (By this time she has developed a formidable reputation for blunt speaking and fiscal vigilance, so much so that many of the organization's younger women are frankly scared of her.)

Major Millen, Buddy Cohen, and Max Wolf grin from an article celebrating the lavish opening of the new Hillvale Country Club, affluent Jewish Knoxville's answer to its chronic exclusion from Gentile high society. "Picture if you please, a magnificent landscaped setting overlooking the river . . . a beautiful mansion luxuriously but artfully furnished," gushes the article. "Fabulous clothes, magnificent jewelry, gorgeous women, orchids by the gross, and men impeccably attired."

Meanwhile, there's a bumper crop of Jewish children. The 1951 issue mentions that the JCC Sunday school, now in its twenty-second year, has a record enrollment of 135 children. (The next year, school enrollment would drop to 100 because of Temple Beth El's reinstitution of its own religious school. However, the Center Sunday school would continue until 1956.)

On page 4 is a roundup of Jewish news from around the world: A paragraph notes that 630,000 immigrants have gone to Israel since independence in 1948; meanwhile, Rabbi Leo Jung of the B'nai B'rith

Institute issues a "stinging rebuke to America's Jewish mothers," demanding they return to marrying for love and "forget the mink coats and fancy rings." Suzy Snoops announces "The kids are off to colleges. Rita Green, Barbara Winick, and Joyce Robinson to Ohio State. Sidney Deitch to Northwestern. Morris Rosenblatt to Penn. Arnold Bucove to Columbia, Eric Chazen to U-T Med. School, Sally Block, Myra Corkland and Pessa Caller to Alabama . . . Shirley Bernard, Pauline Chazen, Norma Shagan, Karl and Harvey Liberman, Wayne Miller, David Weinstein and Lou Woolf will enroll at University of Tennessee." (By my rough count, about a third of these people brought their college degrees back to Knoxville and formed the next generation of community leaders.)

Another column welcomes seven local children from the Zionist camp Tel Yehuda, while other pieces laud the activities of the Knoxville Zionist District (headed by Dr. William Shaw), Hadassah (Knoxville's Mrs. J. B. Corkland is regional president this year), and the Israel bond drive headed by Sam Rosen. Sam and Esther Rosen, both staunch Labor Zionists, had intended to settle in Israel after their scrap iron business in Albany, Indiana, was destroyed by an explosion in the late 1940s. (One of his relatives whispered to me that the immigrant Sam and his brother-partner, Israel, were actually stockpiling some kind of chemicals for use by

Esther Rosen. She and her husband, Sam, were ardent Zionists at the center of Knoxville Zionist activity. Esther started the first local Hadassah directory. Courtesy of Knoxville Jewish Federation.

Several Knoxville teens attended this Young Judaea Convention in 1949. Courtesy of Barbara Winick Bernstein.

Knoxville's junior Zionists posed at 1946 Young Judaea banquet. Only about a half dozen of those pictured still live in the area. Courtesy of Barbara Winick Bernstein.

the underground Israeli army when the whole works went up in smoke. I couldn't get Esther and Sam Rosen to comment on this.) The serious illness of their son Allan, who died many years later of a rare congenital disease, made them reluctant to trust the still-primitive medical facilities in Israel. Instead, the Rosens bought a scrap yard in Knoxville, competing fiercely in the business world with existing scrap dealers Buddy Cohen and Max Kesselman. According to their grandson Stephen, that competition extended to the annual Israel bond drives launched by the Knoxville Jewish leadership after statehood was achieved. "The first year they moved here, Sam and Esther gave a contribution that substantially upped the ante among Knoxville businessmen," he told me. I couldn't find financial records of those first campaigns, but pledge booklets from the late 1950s and 1960s show scrap iron magnates Kesselman, Cohen, and Rosen among the top twenty contributors. In any case, the Rosens quickly became prominent in local Zionist affairs. Esther Rosen was chapter president of Hadassah in 1951 and created the first local Hadassah Directory the next year. Sam poured his energies into fundraising for Israel and later was a delegate to the first convention of AIPAC, Israel's political lobby in Washington. "Melvin Goldberger from the Temple flew Sam up there in his private plane," Esther says. "This community was always very involved with Israel."

Another notable contribution was made after Sam Rosen passed his first Yom Kippur at the old Heska Amuna synagogue on Fifth Avenue. Apparently, the *shul* had to keep its windows open because of the early autumn heat—a notable feature of High Holy Days in the South. All day long the smell of frying bacon fat from a nearby restaurant wafted in to beleaguer the fasting Jews inside. Figuratively fed up with this situation, Sam and brother Israel Rosen donated funds for an air-conditioning system so the windows could stay closed.

Knoxville Jews were thrilled on May 6, 1951, by a sudden visit from Israeli Prime Minister David Ben-Gurion, who came on a tour of TVA facilities at the behest of rising industrialist Guilford Glazer. Guilford and his mother, Ida, were the hosts for Ben Gurion, who brought along his minister of labor, Golda Meir, and several top cabinet members. I was amused to see that a report on the event in *The Southern Israelite*, Atlanta's Jewish newspaper, still identifies Golda Meir

David Ben-Gurion (along with Labor Secretary Golda Meir, not pictured) came to Knoxville in 1951. Knoxville-bred industrialist Guilford Glazer organized the visit. Courtesy of Knoxville Jewish Federation.

by her American name, Goldie Meyerson. The account goes on to describe Guilford Glazer as "a young and extremely capable communal figure" who on only three or four days' notice "undertook to arrange the entire affair single handedly." This not only included rounding up Tennessee's top officialdom and Jewish leaders from all surrounding areas but also footing the bill for the entire affair. Knoxville Jewry turned out by the hundreds for a dinner at the Farragut Hotel on South Gay Street. Gov. Gordon Browning came, along with Congressmen Howard Baker and Albert Gore. Southern Zionist leaders showed up in force, hosted on the podium by regional Zionist Organization of America president Ben Winick and southern region of Hadassah president Mrs. Jacob Corkland. Joe Goodstein tells me that since his father, Ben, hailed from the same Polish town—Plinsk— as the famous prime minister, the two spent some time reminiscing. In later years, Knoxville would receive visits from several other Israeli luminaries, including Yitzhak Rabin, Abba Eban, and Moshe Dayan.

⧜

Somewhere among the various New Year's greetings in the back pages of the 1952 *Menorah* my eye is caught by a small ad that reads "Compliments of THE BERKLINE CORP., MORRISTOWN, TENN, Mr. And Mrs. Lester Popkin and Family." It's an early marker for what was happening an hour east of Knoxville in a small community called Morristown. By the 1930s, a few Jewish merchant families from Middlesboro and nearby communities had started businesses in Morristown, some catering to workers on the new TVA projects. Northeastern Jews in the textile industries began to arrive, most often looking to start factories with cheaper, nonunion labor. Abe and Sadie Hirschfield came down from Patterson, New Jersey, to start a silk mill, along with their nephew Jerry Gerson. His brother Seymour Gerson went into the mountains to buy the pelts of small animals such as skunks. These pelts were processed, made into strips, and sent to the spinning industries in North Carolina to reduce static electricity in machinery. During World War II both Gersons began furniture businesses. By this time, a handful of Jewish-owned furniture factories and related businesses were quickly becoming the heart of Morristown's industry, and its salvation from the economic doldrums that plagued so many small southern towns. Once again, the need for cheap land and nonunion labor pushed the manufacturers south. The Gluck brothers from Brooklyn started one of the first furniture companies in the 1930s, followed at the end of the decade by Jacob and Lester Popkin from Springfield, Massachusetts. Jacob went back to Springfield, but Lester stayed on to run the Berkline Corporation, whose well-known recliners became ubiquitous in American living rooms during the postwar period. Others, like the Solod family from Springfield, started feeder industries that supplied processed materials to the big furniture concerns. These were big-time manufacturers oriented toward northeastern cities and national markets. As such, they brought a new element of affluence into the Knoxville Jewish community.

Most of the Morristown crowd joined the Temple, carpooling in for Sunday school and Friday night Sabbath services. Still, Morristown remained a discrete little Jewish community of its own, growing each year as Jewish-owned factories brought down Jewish managers from manufacturing centers in the northeast. Records show less than a dozen of these Morristown families in 1952, but their numbers grew steadily during the next fifteen years.

In many ways, the scientists of Oak Ridge and the big-time manufacturers of Morristown represented the wedge end of things to come. In Knoxville, as all over America, Jewish young people were going off to college in record numbers and Jewish families were becoming more affluent. The homey but cramped quarters of downtown no longer fit their style. The station wagon trains were rolling west, and the close-knit little community was about to be dispersed. ∽

Six

The Good Old *Days*

Natalie Levison Robinson and I are having a good time browsing around in the Knoxville Jewish Federation's Archives of the Jewish Community of Knoxville and East Tennessee. The name of this archive is a lot grander than its environment, which is a tiny, windowless office above the kitchen and bath showroom of her family's Modern Supply Company in west Knox County. Former Knoxville Jewish Federation (KJF) president Barbara Winick Bernstein pioneered the historical collection in the 1980s, about the same time she, Natalie, and the late community activist Marilyn Shorr began recording oral histories from prominent older members of the community. The new KJF archives committee induced people to send in all sorts of marvelous odds and ends, from family photos to the cryptic minutes of long-ago board meetings. Here's one from August 5, 1888:

> To the Congregation Beth El
> We the undersigned Trustees
> Respectfully submit our Report as follows:
>
> 5 Shares in B & L (Building and Loan) Assoc.
> Paid up dues on same to Oct.
>   1 Sefer Torah cost 100.00
>   1 Shofar 5.00
>   1 Set Prayer Books 5.00
>   1 Wardrobe 25.00

1 Lot Sunday School Books
1 Set lecture Books for Holidays
and Cemetery in good order

(signed) Trustees
H. Spiro
L. David

In one corner, there's a large mounted souvenir map showing downtown Knoxville businesses in the 1920s, clearly showing that Jews didn't have much of a presence on South Gay Street in that decade. Next to it is a whole stack of oversize scrapbooks made by teenage B'nai B'rith girls in the 1970s. There are deeds to houses in the old Jewish neighborhoods of north Knoxville, crumbling citizenship documents, eulogies read at the funerals of several Jewish University of Tennessee professors, and endless newspaper clippings of well-dressed people grinning for the camera. The Robinson family graciously agreed to store all this stuff until the distant time that KJF manages to set up a historical library. Dedicated volunteers such as Jill Weinstein (Myra Corkland Weinstein's daughter-in-law) have gradually wrestled some of these material into neat files—but even more is heaped on tables and in boxes like the goods in a bargain sale.

Today I'm interested in the 1950s and 1960s, so I pick through a carton that seems to date from that era. On top is a newspaper clipping from the Ben-Gurion visit in 1951, clipped improbably to a kid's bar mitzvah announcement and the program from a Rabbi Isaac Winick AZA Sweetheart Dance. Underneath that layer, much to Natalie's surprise, is her own wedding portrait from April 1951, glued to a cardboard thank-you note that bears the printed inscription "Both of us want to thank you sincerely for the gift and for the good wishes!" The bride wears a fitted cocktail-length gown with the small waist and full skirts of the postwar "New Look." She and Mitchell seem very chic. "Now, who ever sent that in?" Natalie muses. I ask her what her life was like in those days, when the Jews at Hillvale Country Club were holding glamorous parties amid the postwar business boom and she mingled with the town's most affluent as a saleslady at Sterling House, her uncle's downtown clothing store. "Well—let's see. Mitchell had just started Modern Supply a couple of years before, with $1,500 in

The wedding picture of
Mitchell and Natalie
Robinson, April 1951.
Courtesy of Knoxville
Jewish Federation and
Mitchell and Natalie
Robinson.

savings. He was drawing $50 a week, and we were mostly living off
the income from my job at Sterling House, also $50 a week. Mitchell's
father died the next year, and his mother had started going blind. It
was a struggle," she adds simply. Several decades later, Modern Supply was a successful business, while Mitchell and Natalie became leading financial contributors and leaders in the community.

The payoff for our morning's work is a foot-high stack of hard
data from the 1950s and 1960s. There are Temple and Synagogue
membership rosters, lists of officers and committee chairmen, population surveys, Hadassah directories full of ads for local businesses—
even Jewish Welfare Fund booklets that show which families were
the biggest givers to the annual fundraising campaign. May the Lord
bless and keep all packrats. Somewhere in this gray hoard of names,
addresses, and dollar figures is the pointillist picture of a Jewish community just beginning to move from its cozy downtown roots into
its sprawling suburban future.

I page through a fat booklet printed in 1957, when the Temple dedicated its new building on Kingston Pike. The acknowledgments provide some notion of who was who in the community at this pivotal
time. Melvin Goldberger, wealthy owner of the Square Supply hardware concern, was president. Other officers were George Finer, Lester
Popkin, Clarence Strasburger, Bernard Silverstein, and Sol Moiger.
Main architect for the structure was Sam Good, who also donated
his services to design "The Building" for the fledgling Oak Ridge
congregation a few years earlier. He and his wife show up frequently
in the pages of the *Center Menorah*, running this event or that fund-
raising drive.

Associate architect on the Temple project is young Joseph
Goodstein from the Synagogue, up-and-coming son of the Orthodox grocer Ben Goodstein. Six years before, he married Marion
Hurvitz, who had moved up from Birmingham to attend the University of Tennessee in 1946, a few months after Joe got out of the
army. She'd been accepted to five or six schools contingent upon
finding a place to lodge. The GI's were filling up all the dormitories,
so she chose Knoxville and moved into her Aunt Mary Corkland's
house on Linden Street. The young coed was immediately swept up
into the warm familial cluster of Jews whose world seemed to revolve
around holidays, the Center, and various rites of kinship. "When I
first arrived, I thought everybody else who was Jewish in this town
was named Robinson," she recalled later. "I remember I was the only
non-Robinson in Dolly Robinson's wedding to Ted Reback." Mary
Corkland and her close friend Clara Goodstein were determined to
link up Marion and Joe, but he had to court her for five years before
she agreed to settle down. (At graduation, her parents offered her the
gift of a car or a trip to Israel. She chose Israel. Later she would
become a Hadassah president, and Joe would be active in fund-raising
for the new state. Later still, they would have children and grandchildren living in the Jewish state.)

Not long after Joe helped design the Temple, Marion took over
as director of the Center nursery school, started by Mrs. Marge Marx,
wife of the Temple's Rabbi Meyer Marx. Despite the social exclusion
of that era, the Center nursery school was highly respected and sought
after by non-Jews, since there were very few nursery schools in town

and the prestigious University of Tennessee Child Development Labs often sent their "overflow" toddlers to the Center. One of Marion's first changes when she assumed the directorship in 1963 was to eliminate celebrations of Easter and Christmas, originally included by Mrs. Marx because more Christian than non-Christian students were enrolled in the school. "I always met with the non-Jewish parents every year and explained our Jewish curriculum, how we taught the children about Shabbat and so on," Marion told me recently. "Still, I remember one year when a parent called me, very puzzled, and asked, 'Did y'all take the kids to the circus the other day?' It turned out his child was talking about the school celebration of *Sukkos* [the Ashkenazic pronunciation of the Jewish harvest holiday in early fall and now more commonly called *Sukkot*]."

I turn a few pages in the Temple dedication booklet. Co-chairmen of the 1957 Temple building committee were Harold Winston—one of the new men from the war era—together with Maurice Konigsberg—a member of the old Knoxville Jewish families. Konigsberg's Aunt Blanche is pictured in the 1917 photo of the Temple's first confirmation class. Of the original families who started the Knoxville Hebrew Benevolent Association after the Civil War, only a handful of descendants remained in 1957: Mayme Goodfriend, a descendant of the culinary Spiros; the Lichts and Levys, descended of Emanuel and Samuel Samuels; and Bessie Lobenstein, descended of the Victor Burger family, at whose home the first monthly minyan was convened.

A paragraph in the booklet mentions how the last confirmation held in the old Vine Avenue Temple building in June 1957 provoked memories of the first one, held in the same spot exactly forty years before. Tucked into the booklet is a *Center Menorah* clipping that shows the five young women of the 1957 class. I fish around in my files for the 1917 photo in order to compare these two images that so neatly bracket the era of downtown Jewish life in Knoxville. On the surface, they look quite similar. The class is still tiny—four confirmands in 1917, five in 1957, all teenaged scions of the Temple's leading families. The girls in white dresses still pose in attitudes of graceful purity, each clutching a bouquet of spring flowers to her bosom. I suppose the ingenues of 1957 look a tad more sophisticated in heavy makeup and curve-hugging, cap-sleeved creations of the sort Audrey Hepburn made famous. Yet the names in the caption show deeper changes since the days when Temple membership was primarily composed of middle-class German merchants. Smiling into the camera is Barbara Popkin, daughter of Eastern European Jews, whose father Lester is making a fortune with his Berkline furniture company in Morristown. Next to her is Renee Lisser, daughter of Holocaust refugees, whose father Steve is a scientist in Oak Ridge. The old split between German Jews and Eastern European Jews has vanished, replaced by an equally deep philo-sophical split between Jews who demand more or less of the tradi-tional rituals. A year earlier, the joint Sunday school at the Jewish Community Center had finally been dissolved, despite the fact that Heska Amuna was in the process of moving away from Orthodoxy toward the middle-ground Conservative movement. Now Temple and Synagogue Jews kept the religious education of their children com-pletely separate. That same year, Heska Amuna broke ground on its new building, located less than a mile away on the same section of Kingston Pike.

Though total Jewish population had not grown much, the rela-tively large number of school-age children probably encouraged each institution to expand. In 1957 the Temple enrolled 95 students (from 120 member families), while a Synagogue list from three years later shows 83 students (from 204 member families). This baby boom pat-tern was even more evident in youthful Oak Ridge, which boasted 100 family memberships and more than 100 students in its religious school by 1960. However, a 1957 survey of Jewish population in Knox-ville found only 772 individuals, evidence that community numbers were continuing to wane as a proportion of total growth in the area. (By contrast, today's Knoxville–Oak Ridge Jewish community claims 1,800 to 2,000 individuals, but its religious school enrollment is about 250—about 50 fewer children than during the peak period four decades earlier.) Another sign of low growth is the 1962 closure of Hillvale Coun-try Club, for there continued to be relatively few wealthy Jews in Knox-ville, and this select group began to shift its priorities to the support of Israel and community needs.

A decline in growth makes it even more remarkable that the late 1950s to mid-1960s saw the construction of impressive new Temple, Synagogue, and Jewish Community Center buildings. How in the world did fewer than one thousand, mostly middle-class Jews manage to do so much? The Temple dedication booklet puts it this way: "It was the need for educational facilities for our youth which inspired our congregation to plan for a new and beautiful Temple Beth El. Yet our dreams would have remained unfulfilled had it not been for Mr. and Mrs. Arnstein, who, in the autumn of 1954, graciously presented the congregation with the means to purchase a lot on Kingston Pike." According to the booklet, the Temple hired a professional fund-raising organization, which managed to meet its goals in a mere six-week campaign during 1955. The Arnsteins ultimately sent about $60,000 for adornments and furnishing, plus another large amount to help the old Center expand next door into the former Temple building on Vine Avenue.

The year after Temple Beth El's move, about thirty people from Knoxville helped Max Arnstein celebrate his one hundredth birthday with a party at the elegant St. Moritz Hotel in New York. When he died in 1961 at age 102, his will left major bequests to the Jewish Community Center, enabling it to purchase a large tract of land for a renamed Arnstein Jewish Community Center on Deane Hill Drive in west Knoxville. Originally, there had been some talk of building a unified campus for a Temple, Synagogue, and Center on the Deane Hill property, but by the time land was purchased, the Temple and Synagogue had already gone their separate but parallel ways.

Temple Beth El and Heska Amuna Synagogue both chose to relocate on the edge of Sequoyah Hills, a tree-lined upper-class neighborhood where some of the most successful Jewish families had moved. During this period, the Sequoyah Hills section of Kingston Pike became Knoxville's Church Row, filling up with half a dozen large sanctuaries constructed in the contemporary style. To be at this location was to be respectable and established—if not socially accepted—among the city's religious denominations.

Five years before, in observance of Brotherhood Week, the ladies of Temple Beth El's sisterhood produced an Interfaith Tea for the schoolteachers of Knoxville and Knox County. In a "Cavalcade of Holidays," nine tables displayed the symbols and ceremonials of the

Youth groups like the Jewish high school fraternity AZA, pictured here with its "sweetheart" in the mid-1950s, were a vital social outlet in a time when Knoxville Jews were often excluded from Gentile social affairs. Courtesy of the author.

major Jewish festivals, along with the recital of prayers for each holiday and traditional hymns sung by the choir. It must have been a very big deal, because the Temple's library has a bound book containing minutes of all the planning meetings, lavish photos of the display tables, and the guest book signed by forty-some local educators. "My goodness, yes," laughed Sylvia Silver when I reminded her of that event. "It seemed like we used to spend hundreds of hours on those sorts of things. Sometimes I look back and wonder why." The Interfaith Tea was a nationwide effort by Reform sisterhoods to raise awareness of Jewish traditions in the public schools. It was pioneered in a pilot program at the Tree of Life Congregation in Columbia, South Carolina. Belinda and Richard Gergel, who authored a rich history of this congregation entitled *In Pursuit of the Tree of Life*, suggest that such events became elaborate social spectacles in the Jewish community as a direct result of nonacceptance by Christian society. "One salutary effect of these exclusionary practices was the direction of great energy and commitment into the temple's programs and activities of other Jewish organizations," the Gergels write. "The annual Interfaith Teas were organizational masterpieces, and even the social events were carried through with meticulous planning."

In the face of this exclusion, Jews in the South not only bonded together socially but also felt a pressing need to present a good outward appearance among the Gentiles. "Growing up in an environment where a majority considered them a people apart left Jews with a pervasive sense of anxiety," writes Leonard Dinnerstein in his 1994 book *Anti-Semitism in America*. "Nevertheless, they managed to survive, thrive, and interact pleasantly with their Christian neighbors. Regional customs dictated a surface cordiality between and among Caucasians. Therefore, by always watching themselves and never engaging in activities that might antagonize members of the dominant society, Jews hoped to avoid public discomfort. Most Southern Jews were obsessed with the need to accommodate to community mores, and they never forgot that they were members of a minority group in an area where outsiders were considered deviant."

By the late 1950s, a few high school social clubs apparently included some Jewish members. However, this seemed to be more the exception than the rule. My impression from dozens of interviews is that most native Knoxville Jews were simply resigned to their position during this era and accommodated by associating almost exclusively with organizations inside the Separate Circle. "Back then, I didn't really have any friends that weren't Jewish," comments Sirkie Billig, an elderly woman who was born and raised in Knoxville. In some ways, involvement with Jewish organizations engineered a kind of "respectable isolation" within the community at large. In the heavily church-going South, one simply had to belong to a religious institution in order to fit in and be credited with good moral character. So insofar as Jews affiliated with Jewish organizations in order to have a social circle and feel more comfortable in a churchgoing town, they were separated even more from Gentile social circles.

Heska Amuna's somewhat larger membership did not seem to spend much organizational time reaching out to its Christian neighbors—perhaps because of its own traditionalism, but more likely, in Natalie

Robinson's words, "because most people at the Synagogue were too busy just making a living." Like the Temple, however, the Synagogue's leadership was motivated by the need to provide classroom space for its growing population of children. Lacking a key financial angel to boost its campaign, the Synagogue relied on a scheme of building fund pledge cards pioneered by the energetic Mrs. Hilda Busch Nisenson, after whom the educational wing is named. For years, her gold-lettered cards adorned with the motto "Let Us Build!" were ubiquitous around the community. The Heska Amuna dedication booklet from 1960 devotes a whole page to this notable woman, of whom so many longtimers speak with a certain awe. "In the Biblical account of the return of our people from Exile in Babylon, it is said, 'Everyone with one of his hands wrought in the work, and with the other hand held his weapon and SO DID THEY BUILD!' We can truly apply this to Hilda, for as she held in her one hand the weapon of pen and Building Fund Card, with the other hand she held aloft her lighted torch of courage and perseverance—never faltering no matter how difficult the task became, working always with kindness and pleasantness to remind each of us to continue to build and to have our hands, also, in the work." One can almost imagine the years of nonstop *noodging* implied in this effusion of praise.

The new location chosen for the Temple and Synagogue acknowledged the shift in Jewish geography. By the mid-1950s up-and-coming Jews were starting to move out of the old, decaying neighborhoods north and east of downtown into the new western suburbs, where farmland was being subdivided into modern housing developments. Sequoyah Hills, arranged around the tree-lined Cherokee Boulevard with its several miles of walking paths adjacent to Fort Loudon Lake, was the newer western equivalent of Fairmont Boulevard in North Knoxville, where affluent Jews moved in the 1920s. The Ben Winick family was one of the first to settle west in Sequoyah Hills. Eventually, the neighborhood included the families of Lester Popkin, Nathan Robinson, Mitchell Robinson, Sam Miller, Joseph Goodstein, Harold Winston, Harry Caller, David Liberman, Harry Busch, Max Morrison, Ida Glazer, Ada Averbuch, Ike and Jake Green, Phillip Chazen, Melvin Goldberger, Max Friedman, Abe Joffe, Herbert Smullian, Abe Ross, and Sam Rosen to state a partial list of prominent Knoxville Jewish families.

In 1960, Heska Amuna children help dedicate the educational wing of the new Synagogue building on Kingston Pike in suburban west Knoxville. At this point in the baby boom, about one-third of the Jewish community was composed of school-age children. Courtesy of Knoxville Jewish Federation.

A few years after the Temple and Synagogue were built, younger or less affluent families began to settle in the middle-class subdivisions of West Hills a few miles from the Synagogue. The bulk of the community still lived east and north for some time thereafter. "When we moved to West Hills, my mother cried because she thought she'd never see us," relates Myra Corkland Weinstein. "Before the interstates were finished, it took an hour to drive between our house and their place east of downtown on Linden Avenue." (In 1961, West Hills was still so remote from banks and other civilized services that a new convenience store in the neighborhood cashed checks and sold license plates!) Within this decade, however, it became home to the Weinsteins, the Lou Joffes, Bernard Bernsteins, Harvey Libermans, Bernard Silversteins, and Allan Rosens, among many others. A large portion of middle-class Knoxville residents did the same. In the next decade, with the advent of WestTown mall and the death of downtown retail business, this neighborhood would become the de facto commercial center of a sprawling suburban city.

Records show that the removal of the Jewish community to west Knoxville occurred with almost dizzying speed. The 1952 Hadassah directory lists 211 members living in Knoxville, out of which only 27 had addresses in west Knoxville (almost all in and around Sequoyah Hills). By 1961 the directory lists 93 members with west Knoxville addresses, of which several dozen are in West Hills. The 1965 directory shows 145 of the 220 Knoxville members with addresses in west Knoxville, and about half in West Hills. By 1970 less than a dozen Knoxville members are outside west Knoxville, and the largest number live in West Hills.

The Knoxville Hadassah directories—which contain ads from most of the area's Jewish businesses—offer a revealing glimpse of how the Morristown "furniture" community grew. ("I always thought you could write a whole history just by looking through these books," says former Hadassah president Lee Miller, who made it her project to gather these old directories for the KJF archives.) Home addresses for Hadassah's female members are listed, along with a "Precious Jewels" page listing minors and grandchildren of members. Members and advertisers from Morristown, which had its own small but very active Hadassah chapter, are listed separately in the directories. Since most but not all Jewish community members joined Hadassah in the heavily Zionist Knoxville–Morristown communities, the directories probably reflect a reasonable minimum estimate of those present at the time.

The 1952 Hadassah directory lists eleven women and nine children in the Morristown section. Five Morristown companies bought ads (Berkline, Minjay Mills, Gluck Brothers, Tennessee Furniture Industries, and Modern Upholstered Chair). In 1961 sixteen women and twenty-seven children are listed, along with ads from six Morristown companies. (Seymour Gerson's Forest Products Corporation and Sam Solod's Morristown Batting Company show up.) At this point, other records show the Temple included a "Morristown representative" on its board, indicating the increasing importance of this little group of families as Temple leaders. In the 1965 Hadassah book, the Morristown total is nineteen women, twenty-seven children, and thirteen company ads (including Morristown Chest Company, Jay Solod's Southern Furniture Supply Company, Mohawk Furniture, the Steinfeld family's Shelby Williams of Tennessee, Laminate Plastics, G. Marcus Jones, General Contractor, and GBC Inc., "Trucking for the Furniture Industry"). This growth seems to have peaked in the late 1960s. The 1967 directory shows twenty-two women, thirty-four children, and sixteen companies; in 1968 there are twenty-five women, forty-three children, and eighteen advertisers, though by this time a few advertisers are clearly Gentile-owned banks and service companies who had reason to court the Morristown Jewish market. Family names listed at this time include three Gerson families, three Gluck families, Gralnik, Gudis, Larimer, Lasnick, Marx, Mehlman, Moss, Steven Popkin, Renert, Rogers, two Schnitman families, Snowiss, two Solod families, Stryer, Taylor, and Wolffe. Many of those clans were related by marriage to each other as well as to families in Knoxville.

In the 1970 edition, the total numbers have all dipped slightly, a trend that continued in the next two decades as the Jews of Morristown retired or sold out of their businesses. Today Morristown's remaining furniture industry is completely owned by non-Jews. My 1999 Hadassah directory includes just one Morristown member, Mrs. Bunny Gerson. (I'm told that two or three other Jewish families are left in the town, including a couple of Jewish doctors who recently located there.)

In late 1998, I interviewed Ursula and Harry Marx, two long-time Morristown residents who had retired to a handsome condominium development in west Knoxville. They lived in Morristown from 1963 to 1984 and raised two daughters, the younger of whom is now a Reform movement cantor living in another state. Sitting around a table in their spacious art-filled living room, they gave me a detailed portrait of the "good old days" in this little affluent satellite to the Jewish Knoxville community. The Marxes came to Morristown in 1963 at the behest of Sam Solod, whose Morristown Batting Company supplied the cotton stuffing for Berkline's upholstered chairs. Solod actually lived in Massachusetts and owned factories in Morristown and

Hickory, North Carolina. Morristown actively solicited furniture businesses from the northeast, offering tax breaks, cheap land, and most important of all, nonunion labor. "When I came down in 1963, the lowest paid worker in the northeast—someone sweeping the floors—was earning $2.60 an hour," Harry Marx relates. "In Morristown they were earning $1.10." (Much to Sam's dismay, his nephew Jay Solod started his own company to make upholstery filling, and the two were estranged. The fortunes of many Morristown businesses rose and fell on the bitter divisions between family members, not to mention the fierce competition between various Jewish-owned furniture companies.) When Sam Solod wanted to switch from cotton batting into the more technical business of making polyurethane foam (later renaming the company Morristown Foam and Fiber) he brought down German immigrant Harry Marx, who was then running a similar factory in Buffalo. In the same way, a dozen other Jewish managers came down from the northeast to work in the Jewish-owned companies. (Kinship also played its part; for example, Harry is a cousin of Manny Steinfeld, who started the Shelby Williams chair manufacturing company.)

About that same time, the Jewish furniture manufacturers of Morristown decided it was time to have a country club where they could entertain business associates in a style appropriate to their rising financial might. Together with American Enka—a Dutch-owned nylon/rayon maker that was the only big Gentile-owned firm in town, they bought a 200-year-old dairy farm and subdivided it into a golf course, clubhouse, and residential lots (the local Hadassah chapter held their luncheons there.) "Of course, if it hadn't been for the Jews starting the Morristown Country Club, they probably wouldn't have gotten in," Harry says wryly. It was a modest affair, with dues of just twenty-five dollars a month when the Marxes arrived. Sam Solod bought several of the residential lots and gave one to Harry and Ursula as part of the deal. They built a house there. "Sam said, 'If you stay five years, it's free, otherwise you pay me back. But when Sam got sick about four years later, he brought us the deed and said, 'You don't owe me anything,'" Harry recalls.

The rabbi from the Temple usually came to Morristown for a Shabbat dinner once a month and conducted services for the twenty-odd families there. Much like the young professional families of Oak

Ridge, Morristown families who had not been active Jews became quite enmeshed in Temple life. "Down here people are very involved with their churches," Ursula explains. "When you suddenly find yourself in a small town among a lot of Baptist people, you become more concerned about your own religion." Important bonding experiences for these young manufacturers and managers in the 1960s were the Morristown carpools, which shuttled their children back and forth to Temple Beth El's Sunday school every week. "We always had a carful—at least five or six," says Ursula. In 1970, Harry Marx became president of the Temple, despite the long commute from Knoxville.

Steve Lisser of Oak Ridge also served a term as president in this era, and the board of trustees included an Oak Ridge representative for a small group of families who preferred to affiliate with a Reform congregation. Meanwhile, the Jewish Congregation of Oak Ridge was growing fast. "The 1950s and 60s saw an influx of a new generation of scientists and engineers," recalls former president Herb Hoffman in the fiftieth anniversary booklet printed by the Jewish Congregation of Oak Ridge (JCOR). "Congregation membership at one time reached almost 100 family units. In 1962, with enrollment in our religious school over 100, we dedicated our Education Wing, but the sanctuary still served as the Social Hall. What work and milling around and impatience as we transitioned from one use to the other after a Shabbat morning bar mitzvah service." Ruth Carey later joked that the sound of moving chairs after a *simcha* was the coda to an Oak Ridge service.

Rabbi Kenneth Bromberg, a Brooklynite who served JCOR from 1958 to 1962, adds these memories from his notes of that time:

> Feel of Oak Ridge is like that of a university town. Lotsa kids in the school for a small congregation . . . "tradition" of calling them in from recess by sounding the shofar . . .
>
> Civil rights period: member of the Mayor's Commission on Civil Rights—negotiations—demonstrations at Davis Brothers Cafeteria—attempt to break the color line at a local movie house; fringe benefits—saw a couple

of movies free . . . Freedom Bus from Memphis on the
way to Oak Ridge to test Holiday Inn. Word sent from
Holiday Inn HQ to Oak Ridge outlet, "Don't fight 'em,
join 'em."

Unspoken deal: congregants naïve about religion,
rabbi a neophyte in science. We would teach each other
with mutual respect personally and for each other's academic discipline. Oh, those wonderful JCOR Off-Broad-
way Jewish themed productions. I loved participating in
them particularly the camaraderie of rehearsals. I played
Tevya at age 32. JCOR [was] an idyllic start to a rabbinic
career.

An important addition to the Oak Ridge community was Mira
Kimmelman, a Holocaust survivor from Danzig who came to Oak
Ridge by way of Cincinnati. (She wrote compellingly of her life in
Europe in *Echoes from the Holocaust: A Memoir*, published by the University of Tennessee Press.) In 1964, Kimmelman's late husband, Max,
employed by Burlington Industries, was transferred to nearby
Rockwood, a small East Tennessee town. Knoxville was fifty-four
miles away, Oak Ridge was thirty-eight—a big difference in those days
before state highway construction was completed. They settled at the
far western edge of Oak Ridge because it was the nearest available
Jewish community, and Max commuted every day for ten years until
his retirement. You'd think Mira would have been miserable in those
first years, a young European immigrant mother stuck all day without
a car in a strange suburban neighborhood, transplanted to a town with
a tiny Jewish community. JCOR had added classrooms by then, but
the building still didn't look like much—just a basic structure with
exposed steel beams and concrete blocks. "It was home from Day One,"
she remembers. "People came and got me, brought me places. The
established Jewish community in Cincinnati did not accept outsiders
so much. Here, everybody was from somewhere else, everybody was a
newcomer. There was no precedent here. The synagogue joined the
Conservative movement but had to accommodate to people with all
sorts of backgrounds." Mira Kimmelman herself had received a thor-
ough European Jewish education. This made her especially precious

The highly professional Oak Ridge congregation grew sharply through Oak Ridge National Laboratory hiring in the 1950s and 1960s. Here, children are dressed in costumes for Purim, the Feast of Lots. Genevieve Shaw Kramer, one of the few area natives, is at the piano. Religious school enrollment in Oak Ridge reached to more than one hundred children in the early 1960s; it has dropped to fewer than thirty students today. Courtesy of Mel and Fran Sturm.

to the growing Oak Ridge congregation, which now had reached its peak enrollment of 150 students. She taught for thirty-five years, serving as principal for most of that time and now, in retirement, serving as education chair. "In the 1960s, we had very active Hadassah and sisterhood chapters," she recalls fondly. "We had constant dinners, donors, events, parties. Everybody belonged to everything." In later years, Mira focused on the needs of intermarried families and those whose adult members had never had the opportunity for Jewish learning. She became intensely involved in two national Hadassah educational programs. In Oak Ridge, she started Galgalim, a "whole family" approach that teaches basic Judaica to toddlers together with adult family members. In addition to serving at the regional and national levels of the organization, she also pioneered a combined Oak Ridge–Knoxville effort for Ivrit L'Hadassah, a program of one-on-one tutoring in Hebrew for adults.

Any history of a southern Jewish community in the 1950s and 1960s prompts the natural question: What were relations between the Jews and African Americans in that area, and what roles did local Jews play in the civil rights turmoil of this period? Knoxville's story is a bit different from those of many southern towns. Both its Jewish and African American communities are (and always have been) such a numerically tiny percentage of the total population that discernible interactions between them are hard to trace. (Knoxville's African American population has always been low because this area was not an original slaveholding region, and there was never a significant surge in black job opportunity to bring in large numbers after the Civil War.) The race riots of 1919 closed many Jewish shops because they were located in the Vine Street area adjacent to black neighborhoods, but there is no evidence that Jewish vendors were targets of the rioters' vengeance. Jews in the pawn shop and credit clothing businesses dealt with the lower economic spectrum—to which most black citizens were relegated until recent times—but they dealt with a far greater number of poor whites. For the most part, relations between Jews and African Americans were not so commonly that of merchant and customer (as in many southern towns) as that of employer and employee. To judge by anecdotal and photographic evidence, nearly every significant Jewish business of the 1930s and 1940s had at least one black employee in custodial and delivery posts; I'm told the passage of the Civil Rights Act prohibiting job discrimination resulted in better-paying, more visible positions for some of these employees. However, in this regard, native Knoxville Jews were simply following the standard practice of the area, neither more nor less progressive than other downtown merchants. Like most of the middle class, their families employed black domestic workers, and in one instance a longtime caretaker of Heska Amuna synagogue. Undoubtedly, many of these individuals were intimately involved with the goings-on in the Jewish community, but there is little evidence that Jews were equally involved in the African American community.

One reason local Jews never had to make a stand in the civil rights turmoil is that demonstrations arrived in Knoxville rather late and caused much less commotion than elsewhere in the South. After several sit-ins as well as a lawsuit to integrate the schools, Mayor John Duncan simply declared Knoxville an "open city" in all public accommodations. Integration in the federal installation at Oak Ridge proceeded with even less opposition. (Let the record show, however, that northern transplants Esther and Sam Rosen and Rabbi Kenneth and Joanna Bromberg of Oak Ridge participated in those sit-ins. Esther and Sam were also active in a local integrated summer day camp.)

During the late 1990s, Heska Amuna Rabbi Shlomo Levine became friends with the Reverend Harold Middlebrook, one of Knoxville's most influential African American leaders. Middlebrook delivered a sermon at the Synagogue, and Levine was subsequently asked to deliver invocations at Martin Luther King Day celebrations. The Jewish community was surprised and pleased by such overtures— not because formal relations between the two groups had been strained in the past, but simply because they had never previously existed.

In other areas of the civil rights debate, a Yankee Jewish lawyer would put Knoxville squarely in the national news. When Barbara Winick took a post-college trip to New York City to visit her childhood friend Pauline Chazen, she was set up for a blind date with Bernard E. Bernstein, a promising young student from New Jersey. Matters went so well that Barbara promptly moved to New York and took a job writing copy for a fashionable Fifth Avenue department store. The pair married in 1956 and lived in a one-room apartment in Greenwich Village while Bernie attended law school at New York University. After their daughter, Barri, was born a year later, they decided to come south. Bernie transferred his credits to the University of Tennessee and went to work for Dave Blumberg selling life insurance while he attended law school full time. Bernie's mother had died before their move, and he was still saying Kaddish (the memorial prayer recited daily by the observant in the eleven months after the decease of one's parent or close relative, which must be recited in the company of at least nine other Jewish adults). He formed the habit of coming to Heska Amuna's daily minyan, which was held most evenings at the Center or in the basement of Harold's Deli. "With

Attorney Bernard Bernstein rose to state and national prominence through civil rights cases and later came to represent many of Knoxville's leading businesses. Courtesy of Barbara Winick Bernstein.

so many Jewish pawn shops and clothing stores on Gay Street, you could round up merchants as they were closing their stores and make a minyan," Bernie says. "They found out I could *daven* [lead prayers in Hebrew chant] so after I finished saying Kaddish I was still in demand." He couldn't get over how they all spoke the ancient Hebrew prayers with a distinct southern accent. Bernie has fond memories of the older men he met through evening minyans: Lou Joffe of the SLOC Shop was a regular member, kind and well loved by all. He and Bernie became good friends. Another regular was Hymie Slovis, one of the five brothers who ran pawn shops in and around Vine and Gay Streets. The best singer was Babe Fay's father "Uncle" Fred Millen—so called because he had thirty or forty relatives among the various downtown merchant families.

At lunchtime on Gay Street, Bernie walked a different way each day so he could meet new people, both Jewish and Gentile. (The young law student couldn't know yet, but in a few decades he would become one of the first local Jews to be welcomed into the upper levels of

Knoxville society.) He graduated from the University of Tennessee Law School in late 1958 and was licensed in the spring of 1959, the same year his son Mark was born. There were only twenty in his graduating class at the University of Tennessee, of which he was the only Jew. Barbara's father, lawyer Ben R. Winick, didn't encourage him to set up practice in Knoxville, where Jewish lawyers were still a rarity. In any case, few Jews were in the highest rungs of the local business community. There were no Jewish furniture companies, no large Jewish-owned department stores (other than a branch of Atlanta-based Rich's), and almost no Jewish doctors. Ben Winick himself had a substantial practice, but few clients with substantial means. "Anyhow, economically there was no great joy in being a lawyer back in those days," Bernie recalls. Dave Blumberg wanted him to go into the insurance business full time, but, instead, Bernie rented a small space on the same floor of the Hamilton Bank Building where Ben Winick practiced. He set up a card table and chair and started to practice law with less than one hundred dollars in the till. ("Next door to me was a young fellow named Jim Haslam," he says. James Haslam later made his fortune by founding Pilot Oil Corporation, a major Knoxville company.) "I had nothing to do, so I would drive around and visit people," Bernie recalls. "I knew Mitchell Robinson socially, so I paid him a visit one day. On the spot he wrote out a check for one hundred dollars and said, 'There, now you're my lawyer.' It was my first retainer."

Within a decade after this modest beginning, Bernie rose to national prominence by representing civil rights cases. It all began in 1962 when he represented the downtown Gateway Bookstore, which was raided by the Tennessee Bureau of Investigation for stocking allegedly obscene materials (such as *Playboy* magazine) on its shelves. Winning that case, he was asked to address the legislature on this issue. All the public attention he received led to an odd call near the end of the 1960s from someone at the American Sunbathing Association who wanted to challenge recently enacted statutes barring the practice of nudism and nudist resorts. "At first I thought Mitchell Robinson had sent me this guy as a practical joke," Bernie admits. He worked out a winning legal strategy for his new client whereby nobody had to go to jail in order to test the law. The night before the trial, he was stymied about how to begin his opening statement. "Barbara said, 'Why don't you just tell them nudism isn't your cup of tea.' So that's how I opened." It proved to be a fortuitous sound bite. When he got to the courthouse, it was mobbed with reporters and TV cameras. That night, Johnny Carson discussed the case in his monologue. *Time* magazine ran a story with the headline: "Nudism: It's Not His Cup of Tea." The Knoxville case was later included in a standard civil procedures textbook.

Through this early baptism by press and a string of other high-profile cases, Bernie became one of Knoxville's most visible lawyers. In 1968 he was elected the first Jewish president of the local Bar Association. His client list included such major community players as Jim Clayton, the mobile home giant; WestTown Mall; Roddy Coca-Cola Distributors; and Proffitt's Department Store. He taught law school for six years as an adjunct professor, helped start the Knoxville Legal Aid Society, and was elected a delegate to the Tennessee Constitutional Convention. (I suspect Ben Winick would have been truly amazed at his son-in-law's professional rise. Unfortunately, Winick died of a heart attack in 1964 while visiting Israel as vice president of the Zionist Organization of America.)

Despite this rapid rise in professional prominence, social life for a Jewish family such as the Bernsteins was still very much centered around the Separate Circle of Synagogue and Jewish community. Bernie held various offices on the Synagogue and Center boards, becoming chairman of the board at Heska Amuna in 1966; Barbara taught Sunday school, and their children went to the Center nursery school. In 1968 the new Center on Deane Hill Drive opened its swimming pool for the first full summer of activities, and the new building was finished a year later. All summer long it was the place where Knoxville Jews spent their afternoons. By most accounts the whole period of the 1960s was an intensely social time with lots of private parties. (This is not too surprising in a town where Jews still weren't invited to join country clubs, and public restaurants still didn't sell liquor by the drink!)

Now more than ever, Zionism was a unifying force in the community. "The survival of Israel was very important to our lives," says

The 1969 completion of the Arnstein Jewish Community Center building on Deane Hill Drive in west Knoxville underlined the transition of the community from its downtown merchant roots to its suburban professional future. Courtesy of Knoxville Jewish Federation.

Bernie Bernstein. Like most of his generation of Knoxville Jews, he vividly remembers the events of June 6, 1967. "The day after the Six Day War started, we raised $67,000 in about twenty minutes." It was an astounding amount for a Jewish community as small as Knoxville's, which had few really wealthy individuals. "That night we had a rally. It was a euphoric moment. People came out of the woodwork—many of the Jewish University of Tennessee professors who had started to come in the 1960s but had never identified with the community, suddenly you heard from them."

Joe Goodstein was chairman of the United Jewish Appeal that year. (His wife, Marion, was president of the Knoxville chapter of Hadassah.) Joe had just gotten back from a UJA briefing in New York when the war broke out. "We had huge attendance at our rally. There was so much excitement in the whole city. I had people—Gentiles— come to me in my office, shake hands with me and say 'This is for OUR people' and I'd be left with a hundred-dollar bill in my hand."

"I was touched because a number of non-Jews came to my office to give me money for Israel," Bernie Bernstein agrees. "The book *Exodus* had a great impact. People were reading it in their offices and calling me up with questions." That Halloween he even saw a friend of his daughter's trick-or-treating as Moshe Dayan, complete with eye patch.

"After 1967, Jews were accepted much better in this community," adds Joe Goodstein. Like many Jews raised in the region, he tends to see that year as a sort of watershed in relations between Jewish and Gentile southerners. "There was so much respect for what the Jews had done in Israel, so much pride." He feels it trickled down to the everyday interactions between Jew and Gentile in business as well as social life.

Historians disagree about how much effect Israel's victory had on southern Gentile feelings toward Jews. As we shall see in the following chapters, the events of 1967 coincided with other forces already at play in southern cities. Within a decade, the rising might of southern universities, high-tech companies, and research centers would dramatically alter Jewish populations in the South and permanently help to change the social status of Jews within the greater community. ∽

Seven

A Snapshot *of* Changing *T*imes

O n the shelves of Heska Amuna Synagogue's library is a thick, gray paperbound tome entitled "A Study of Communality in the Jewish Community of Knoxville, Tennessee." This book is the 1972 master's thesis of University of Tennessee students Shmuel Robinson and Barry Tuchfeld. Tuchfeld is a southern Jew; Israeli citizen Shmuel Robinson (who, remarkably, is quite unrelated to the sprawling Knoxville Robinson clan) happens to be kin by marriage to Mary Linda Schwarzbart. In 1971 the authors extensively interviewed a sample of one hundred families—more than a third of the total population—randomly selected from a list of Knoxville Jewish organizations. The sample members were questioned about their geographic and educational backgrounds, religious observance, social relationships with fellow Jews, experiences in the surrounding Gentile community, and attitudes toward intermarriage. The goal was to explore what types of social and cultural bonds connect a small Jewish community living in a heavily non-Jewish area.

Sift through the powder-dry prose of this work and you find a fascinating statistical portrait of Knoxville Jewry at the point its community dynamics were about to change most drastically. The shift in population—from a small knot of merchant clans to a larger group of unrelated professional families—was already in its early stages. The downtown businesses were disappearing, but old merchant families still accounted for roughly two-thirds of the Jewish population. The newer one-third of the community was dominated by the rapidly arriving force of university faculty and technical researchers, but the deluge of medical doctors was still to come. The newer arrivals seem to have quickly fallen in with the old patterns of the Separate Circle. They formed their closest relationships with other Jews and had little social involvement outside the group. However, they expressed far more dissatisfaction with the prescribed Jewish place in Gentile society. Throughout the study—made at a point when these Southern social barriers were just about to crumble—one gets a foreshadowing of just how much this onslaught of Yankee professionals would contribute to a new social order in Gentile-Jewish relations.

Change was in the air all over the South, where the size and character of small Jewish communities had begun transformations that would be strikingly evident within a decade. Lee Shai Weissbach has traced the population shifts in what he calls "triple digit" southern Jewish communities—that is, smaller cities which contained between 100 and 1,000 Jews in the time between the two World Wars. Knoxville is one of these cities, having maintained a population of 600 to 700 Jews during this period. Weissbach writes that "a great many of the quintessential small communities of the pre–World War II era lost their old character, either because they developed into more substantial Jewish centers or because they went into decline." Of the 104 triple-digit Jewish centers identifiable in 1927, 19 had been transformed by the early 1980s into more significant communities with populations above 1,000 and expanded Jewish infrastructures. (This was the case, for example, in Orlando and St. Petersburg, Florida; Lexington, Kentucky; Charlotte and Raleigh, North Carolina; Columbia, South Carolina; Austin, Texas; and Roanoke, Virginia.) On the other hand, in the same period about one-third of the triple-digit communities of 1927 had seen their Jewish populations drop below 100. Furthermore, of the fifty-one triple-digit Jewish communities of 1927 that still had between 100 and 1,000 Jews five or six decades later, about half had diminished in size. The downward spiral was so pronounced that the Museum of the Southern Jewish Experience was founded in the past decade near Jacksonville, Mississippi, for the express purpose of preserving the history and ritual objects of the South's vanished Jewish populations, where, in the poignant words of that museum's brochure, the southern Jewish experience "survives only as a cherished memory."

The small southern Jewish communities that bucked this trend and grew substantially in the 1960s and 1970s did so for two primary reasons: New Jewish population either formed around expanding industrial centers or around expanding university/research centers. Knoxville falls into this second group, and by 1971 its formerly stagnant population had already begun to increase. Heska Amuna showed 290 families in its roster (up from 204 in 1960) while Temple Beth El had 161 families (up from 120 in 1957). Of course, the entire city was growing, and Jews still account for less than 0.6 percent of Greater Knoxville's total population.

From about 1960 to 1980, postwar efforts to improve higher education in the South were in high gear. All over the region, state and federal dollars were being poured into ambitious projects that aimed to make formerly second-class southern universities into powerhouses that could compete with prestigious northern schools for the best faculty and research. This was the era that produced the academic flowering of such colleges as the University of Florida, Georgia Tech, and the University of North Carolina, among dozens of others. Back in Knoxville, 1963 was the watershed year in which the University of Tennessee began a massive urban renewal project, eventually spreading new buildings over more than 135 acres to the west of its former campus. "Urban renewal made a spectacular growth in enrollment feasible," write James Montgomery, Stanley Folmsbee, and Lee Seifert Greene in *To Foster Knowledge: A History of the University of Tennessee, 1794–1970*. When Marion Goodstein attended the University of Tennessee in 1946, there were only 5,000 students. By 1970 there were 22,844 on the Knoxville campus alone, and by a decade later that number had risen to 38,400. Efforts to increase the academic quality of the university were equally vigorous. Between 1953 and 1963, the University of Tennessee more than doubled its library holdings (from less than 300,00 volumes to more than 600,000). The following year, the University of Tennessee was finally given permission to establish a chapter of the prestigious intellectual fraternity Phi Beta Kappa after being rebuffed for many decades by the national organization. Bold new cooperative programs with the nearby Oak

Ridge National Laboratory were introduced, paving the way for such enterprises as an interdisciplinary graduate school of biomedical sciences. With these and dozens of other new initiatives, the University of Tennessee began to attract large numbers of bright young faculty trained at prestigious universities outside the South.

It was almost a foregone conclusion that a wave of prestigious academic hiring would bring more Jews to Knoxville. The movement of Jews into academia accelerated sharply after World War II as rising expectations and financial programs such as the GI Bill made going to college the standard aspiration for almost every Jewish child. Other catalysts for change were the civil rights movement and the 1964 Civil Rights Act, which made employment discrimination illegal and made ethnicity in all forms more acceptable. Ivy League quotas in college admissions were gone; gentlemen's agreements to discriminate were no longer politically correct. In this more open environment, Jews were free to excel in the nation's most prestigious universities. When they did, eager up-and-coming universities such as the University of Tennessee were more than thrilled to bring these bright young stars to the South.

The Jewish professors who arrived in this wave of hiring had a substantial impact on the university as well as in the tiny Jewish community. Among the first to rise was Larry Silverman, a former dean of the College of Liberal Arts, who was appointed the first vice chancellor of the newly merged statewide University of Tennessee system. In the psychology department alone, ambitious growth brought in a half dozen new professors such as Howard Pollio and Leonard Handler. There had not been a single Jewish professor at the University of Tennessee Law School when Bernard Bernstein and Norbert Slovis had attended; suddenly in the late 1960s, influential Jewish law professors such as Don Wechstein began to arrive, later followed by Neil Cohen. Jewish professors also began to show up in political science and the various physical sciences. (Among prominent arrivals was the late Arthur Brown, who headed the microbiology department and later established the Arthur and Elaine Brown Fund for Microbiology, an endowment fund for the advance of research in this area. He later brought in Jeffrey Becker, whose academic achievements have been matched by his vigorous community work within the Knoxville Jewish

Federation, particularly in the establishment of the Knoxville Jewish Community Family of Funds.) Eventually, Jewish professors headed the University of Tennessee Libraries, the College of Social Work, and numerous other University of Tennessee programs.

Meanwhile, the University of Tennessee Medical Center greatly expanded its research efforts, drawing prominent doctors such as hematologist Amoz Chernoff and oncologist Alan Solomon. "A lot of these guys were young, just raising families, and they had good Jewish backgrounds," Bernie Bernstein relates. "Amoz Chernoff's father had been a Jewish educator, and later Chernoff became chairman of our [Heska Amuna] Board of Education. It was a big improvement to the Sunday school, and a lot of mothers got involved." University of Tennessee psychology professor Howard Pollio (who attended a New York yeshiva in his teenage years) served as volunteer principal of the religious school from 1963 to 1968. He has been followed in more recent decades by highly trained education professionals such as Marilyn Liberman and Nancy Becker at Heska Amuna and Rona Simon and Avigail Rashkovsky at Temple Beth El.

At the time of the Robinson-Tuchfeld study in 1971, medical research had not yet stimulated growth of health care organizations and private practices. Nonetheless, "While there are only a few Jewish lawyers and doctors in Knoxville, the majority of the sample reported that they selected them for professional services," the study reports.

One of the most intriguing aspects of this study is the body of questions it asks about social acceptance of Knoxville Jews in Gentile society. We know in retrospect that attitudes toward Jews began to shift sometime in the 1970s. At least two country clubs in town admitted some Jews, and private social institutions were also loosening up. However, that amazing, rapid sea change—which many longtimers attach to the 1967 war—doesn't seem to have reached most levels of the Jewish community in 1971. About 65 percent of the sample reported experiencing some discrimination. Examples reported in the interviews included both social and economic types of discrimination. Job discrimination was only occasionally reported—perhaps because the 1964 Civil Rights Act and other laws against overt employment discrimination had been in force long enough to reach Knoxville. Yet examples of social discrimination were numerous. The interviewees often told of being excluded from local country clubs and membership selection in local "auxiliaries" and from other prestigious social clubs of the city. Many also expressed concern about discrimination toward their children. Most often this appeared to take the form of being passed over by social fraternities, sororities, and other such groups. It seems the new arrivals felt this exclusion even more keenly than the older merchant crowd: "Those persons with advanced academic education and with a professional occupation either encountered more discrimination or were more sensitive to discrimination both to themselves and to the Jewish community at large," the study reports.

One reason may be that the older families had become fairly resigned to this exclusion over the years, even if they continued to mutter among themselves. When a real problem came up—say, the White Citizens Council making some kind of inflammatory pronouncement—the downtown Jews tended to intervene quietly, behind the scenes. Robinson and Tuchfeld probe further concerning what they call "the community's hesitancy to expose itself as a political entity." Despite feeling discrimination, "most of the respondents said that 'they would rather not go some place where they were not wanted rather than force someone to accept them.'" Only fourteen households in the sample indicated any interest in organizing political action to express their discontent. Two had actually tried to initiate such a move, while the remaining twelve felt such activity should be limited to selected issues "deemed crucial to the majority of the Jewish community." One example of such a "majority" issue mentioned in the study was the 1971 rally of some five hundred Jews who marched from Temple Beth El to Heska Amuna Synagogue to protest the oppression of Jews in Russia. They could march for Jews living elsewhere but felt far less willing to agitate for themselves.

According to the Robinson and Tuchfeld study, Jewish Knoxville's response to social discrimination reinforced communal bonds—even as new arrivals diffused the original bonds of kinship. Women in particular still tended to restrict their activities to Jewish organizations, possibly because in 1971 so few of them had forged contacts with the Gentile community by working outside the home. Almost 90 percent of the sample reported their closest friendships were with other Jews. Moreover, a much higher percentage of Knoxville Jews maintained affiliation with Temple and Synagogue than in other cities of comparable size—only 15.3 percent were unaffiliated, despite a declining pattern of religious observance and increasing rates of intermarriage. Thus, "the community does *not* appear to have taken on large-scale primary relationships with the core society," say the authors. "Those who intermarry and stay within the community [merely] conform to the socio-religious communal way of life." In other words, new members who join the tribe are treated just like family, so long as they take on the same attitudes of sticking primarily with the group.

"The umbilical rope that kept Jews from being totally assimilated during their long and tenuous history still remains. However, internal and external forces have given that rope a new shape," the authors conclude. "Rather than being a tightly braided rope founded on religious convictions, the rope is now a complex network of filaments that represent social, cultural, and ethnic attachments." ∞

Eight

Inside Out
and
Outside In

otes, October 24, 1999. I'm watching a crowd of noisy children move through the halls of Heska Amuna on a Sunday morning, just before the 10 A.M. buzzer rings for the start of religious school. Today's membership rolls show about 650 families (roughly about 2,000 individuals) in the Knoxville–Oak Ridge area, of which about 250 are children enrolled in one of the three religious schools. (Aging Oak Ridge, now filled with retirees, has changed most in the past three decades. Whereas its religious school had an enrollment of more than 100 in the 1960s, that number has now dropped to about 25 children.)

At Heska Amuna, as in Temple Beth El down the street, Sunday is the busiest day of the week. The crowd at religious school tends to be larger than the crowd that comes for Shabbat services on Friday night or Saturday, because education tends to be far more important than prayer to most Jewish parents. From third through seventh grade (the typical year of becoming bar or bat mitzvah), Synagogue children also attend religious school for two hours after school on Tuesday and Thursday afternoons. The Temple children attend one extra day per week from the fourth grade through bar or bat mitzvah. After that, both groups drop back down to one day per week through confirmation at about age sixteen.

Here, as at the Temple, children are dropped off at the front portals by a long stream of carpooling parents. Population has moved farther and farther west since that first wave of migration in the 1950s and 1960s. Most people still live within a half-hour commute from the Synagogue, Temple, and Center, but they are scattered over a twenty-mile stretch of suburban subdivisions that lie west of downtown Knoxville along either side of Interstate 40. In this respect, they mirror the bulk of the county's more affluent population, which has increasingly moved outside the city proper in search of newer houses in finer subdivisions with better views of the lakes and mountains. Not long ago, a Jewish professional couple who moved here from Denver tried to convince the wife's elderly parents to join them in Knoxville. The parents, both European refugees, asked the obvious question: "*Nu*, so where's the Jewish neighborhood for us to move to in this town?" Their children had to admit there was no such thing. These days, it would be difficult to find two dozen Jewish families who live within walking distance of one another. In any case, most of west Knoxville and west Knox County have no sidewalks! It's a pick-'em-up-drop-'em-off culture, radically different from the cozy days when Jewish children could hop a bus and stroll down for a pickle on credit at Harold's Deli before going to shoot hoops at the Center.

The kids at Heska Amuna start the day by gathering in the A. J. Robinson and Sylvia Chapel for a brief *shachrit* (morning service) before heading noisily to their classrooms in the Hilda Nisenson Education Wing. The names of old Synagogue families are on plaques all over the Synagogue, but living descendants are harder to spot on an average Sunday school day. This particular morning, Eli and Asher Robinson are the only scions of old merchant stock sitting in the chapel named for their great-grandfather. Most of the others belong to our newest breed of Knoxville Jews, born to parents who came here after 1970. Lingering out in the hall among several rising bar and bat mitzvah students is Meredith Goldman, whose father, Mitch, is a groundbreaking transplant surgeon at the University of Tennessee hospital. Inside the chapel I see Ellen Iroff, whose parents are both educators in the Knox County school system. She sits near Owen Littman and Rachel Zemel, children of University of Tennessee professors. Others are the offspring of Oak Ridge engineers, government administrators, social workers, lawyers, accountants, and doctors—lots of doctors.

Children perform a Hanukkah program at the Arnstein Jewish Community Center preschool. The Jewish population in Knoxville has more than doubled in the past five decades, boosted in part by an influx of university faculty, scientists, and doctors. Courtesy of Knoxville Jewish Federation.

Looking around this room of squirming *daveners*, I remember an incident from last Yom Kippur. An elderly man—himself a physician as well as the father and father-in-law of two other Heska Amuna physicians—suddenly collapsed. He was taken to the rabbi's study, where within minutes the room literally became crowded with various doctors coming to his rescue. One more physician rose from his pew to join this group but was held back by his wife, who assessed the situation with a practiced eye. "Sit down, man," she told him. "You're a neurologist and this doesn't look like a stroke." The patient recovered, assisted in part by Synagogue doctors who called ahead to the University of Tennessee hospital to smooth his admissions process. "When you're sick in this town," a Synagogue friend joked to me once, "it really helps to be Jewish." In all seriousness, her comment reflects the very real bonds of communal responsibility that still link this community, even now that kinship has ceased to be much of a factor. Interestingly, not a single doctor in that room was raised in Knoxville, and none were related to the old merchant families. Yet the pattern of community formed by those original connections is with us still.

In 1941 the Knoxville–Oak Ridge–Morristown area was home to fewer than eight hundred Jews, and all but a tiny handful belonged to closely related merchant families. In 1999 the descendants of these families constitute a small minority of the approximately eighteen hundred Jews living in this area. Exact proportions are impossible to obtain, but I paged through the names in the current directory for Heska Amuna Synagogue, where I'm most familiar with the branches of family groups. Out of some two hundred fifty family memberships, I found only forty-two that were related to the pre–World War II merchant families. Quite a few of these descendants are now elderly members whose children live elsewhere. As in most southern towns, Knoxville-area Jews hail primarily from the North and Midwest.

Now, only a tiny handful—by my rough count fewer than thirty individuals out of some two thousand Jews now living in the area—currently own or operate as partners in any sort of private business in Knoxville, Oak Ridge, or Morristown. The current list (culled out of Synagogue, Temple, and Hadassah directories as well as general sources) includes the following:

> Crib 'n' Carriage (Milfords)
> Markman's Diamond Brokers (Markman)
> Mill Outlet (Abrams)
> Agri-Feed and Pet Supply/Pet Supply Warehouse (Sturm)
> Hutch Manufacturing Company (Oleshansky)
> Goody's (Robert Goodfriend, CEO—publicly traded)
> Harold's Kosher-Style Food Center (Shersky)
> Star Sales (Foster)
> Modern Supply (Robinsons)
> Paper Paraphernalia (Kay Leibowitz)
> Stephen's Audio Video (Hirschhaut)
> Tennessee School of Beauty (Adam Brown)
> Dixie Barrel and Drum Company (Millen)
> Fay Portable Buildings (Fay)

Kitten Sittin' (Robin Brown)
Calligraphy by Marla (Marla Brody)
Kosher Catering (Marilyn Burnett)
Kosher Karry-out/Challah Kitchen (Marion Goodstein)
M. Licht & Son, Inc. (Richard Licht)
Graftek (Richard and Chris Zemel)

The true percentage of merchants is even smaller, for in many of these family businesses listed above, the primary breadwinner holds some sort of professional job. Exact numbers are difficult to obtain without a current census, but it's a fair guess that at least 95 percent of Knoxville's non-retiree Jewish families include at least one doctor, dentist, accountant, lawyer, college professor, public school teacher, engineer, computer expert, psychologist, health care worker, or social services professional.

Two intriguing stand-outs on the list of businesses above are Markman's Diamond Brokers and Goody's retail clothing stores. Harold Markman came to Knoxville in 1972 as a representative for Zales, one of the big chains that were starting to replace small Jewish-owned jewelers in Knoxville. Four years later he and his wife, Ida, started the first of three Markman's stores, now located in two Knoxville locations and in Chattanooga. Their son Steven is president of the business, while Ida serves as vice president and Harold as CEO. Though Markman's is an independent competing against the chains, it keeps costs low by buying direct from suppliers in Europe and America. Markman's is the only business in town that not only closes on the High Holidays but advertises this fact with a yearly newspaper ad. The store in Chattanooga also closes, even though no Markman family member runs it. "If I had fifty stores, they'd all be closed on Rosh Hashanah and Yom Kippur," says Harold Markman. "If I needed those two days to make a living I'd be in big trouble."

On the opposite end of the retail spectrum is Goody's Clothing, an economy-priced fashion chain with nearly three hundred stores across the South and West. The first member of the family in the economy clothing business was Mike Goodfriend, whose father owned Goodfriends, a men's clothing store in rural Athens, Tennessee. While still working in his father's store, Mike Goodfriend began his Athens

Clothing Outlet in one room above the city jail. It grew to a string of outlets by the time his son Robert (educated at an East Coast college) was ready to take over in the 1970s. The chain was renamed Goody's as it made the transition from seconds and overruns to budget-priced high-fashion clothing. Robert Goodfriend headquartered the store just outside Knoxville in the early 1980s, and it went public within the decade. Robert Goodfriend is now CEO. Both the Goodfriend and Markman families belong to Temple Beth El.

Despite these two notable exceptions, 1970–80 was the pivotal time when the older, smaller Jewish businesses of Knoxville disappeared as the largest wave of Jewish professionals moved in. At the same time as the University of Tennessee was expanding, federal research dollars allowed the Oak Ridge laboratory complex to hire a significant number of new young scientists (such as my own husband, Ted, who heads a research group in materials science). The growth and increasing sophistication of medical research at local hospitals also stimulated efforts to attract more board-certified physicians in a large number of specialties. On the heels of this expansion came more health care organizations and social welfare agencies, which often tended to attract the secondary breadwinners in many Jewish professional families. I have heard this process facetiously called "medical chain migration."

Meanwhile, people moved west, the suburban shopping centers went up, and downtown businesses closed. In many cases, Jewish business owners led this trend, either because they sniffed the wind or because various members of the merchant generation were nearing retirement age anyway. "When WestTown Mall opened [in the 1970s] it all changed downtown. We finally closed down a year or two before the World's Fair in '82," says ninety-four-year-old Dora Green, whose husband, Ike, and brother-in-law Jake were partners in Green's Hardware at the north end of Gay Street as well as an auto sales concern. Since the children had long since grown and moved away, the parents simply sold out their stock and retired to a comfortable life in Sequoyah Hills. "The story of Jews in the South," Eli Evans argues in *The Provincials*, "is the story of fathers who built businesses to give to their sons who didn't want them. It is a drama played over and over again thousands of times across the South." Perhaps so, but the Knoxville

During the 1970s, the exclusion of Knoxville Jews from Gentile
social circles largely disappeared. In 1984 councilman Max Friedman's
daughters Selma Smullian and Lillian Epstein attended the opening
of an interstate overpass named in honor of the prominent jeweler/
politician. Courtesy of Scott Hahn.

Jewish equation worked a little differently. In this town, most businesses were small, and there was rarely enough to split between more
than one sibling. Small grocers or pawn shop owners didn't necessar-
ily want the same kind of futures for their sons. People sent their kids
to college in hopes they would find a better way of life.

To that end, scores of local kids took their college degrees and
went off to seek broader horizons. (Three from prominent Knoxville
Jewish families joined the rabbinate: Lynn Liberman, a Conservative
rabbi, is the daughter of Harvey and Marilyn Liberman and granddaughter of David Liberman; the others are Geela Rayzel Raphael,
daughter of Mitchell and Natalie Robinson, who was ordained at the
Reconstructionist seminary; and Joe and Marion Goodstein's son

David, an Orthodox rabbi in Israel.) I've met very few of these colle-
giate émigrés, but I can walk down the hallway at Heska Amuna, where
old religious school pictures are hung, and pick out most of the kids
who stayed. Arnold Cohen, Scott Hahn, Larry Leibowitz, and Doug
Weinstein became attorneys; Mary Beth Leibowitz is a Knox County
criminal court judge married to neurologist Dr. Michael Eisenstadt.
Arnold Schwarzbart, son of an immigrant tailor, worked for thirteen
years as an architect, then began his career as a Judaica artist whose
ceramic work and large-scale art installations appear in homes, synagogues, and other Jewish institutions around the country. Other children of local merchants include a psychotherapist, an architect, a few
podiatrists, a dentist, and one or two accountants. Alexia Levison, a
great-grandchild of boardinghouse-operator Fanny Levison, is now
press secretary to Tennessee Governor Sundquist, while David Balloff,
the grandson of small-town merchant Lou Balloff, works on the staff
of Congressman John Duncan.

Jewish professionals continued to flow into the area for another decade,
just as they flowed into other university towns across the south. Leonard
Dinnerstein has estimated that more than 80 percent of today's southern Jews do not originally hail from that region. In Knoxville, this
process has more than doubled the total Jewish population in the past
thirty years. Temple and Synagogue became roughly equal in total
numbers as well as in the educational-financial profile of their members. Still, the old legacy of kinship connections, overlaid with the
diverse geographic backgrounds of members, gives Knoxville Jewish
life a distinctive flavor. Newcomers often remark on the curious mix
of small-town warmth and urban sophistication that is so much a part
of this community. "People used to move to the area because they had
a relative here," says Mary Linda Schwarzbart. "Now the educational
level is much higher, and they come to the area for jobs. It changes
how the Jewish community needs to function. Jewish friends end up
creating their own extended families because sharing life-cycle celebrations is so important to us."

At the same time, Knoxville Jews have become much more
involved in the outer arena of Knoxville life than they were thirty

years ago. Discrimination has by no means disappeared, but it has ceased to be much of a force in determining the civic and social involvement of Jewish community members. "You get a lot of pushes and pulls for your volunteer time, for your financial support, for your attendance," says Rody Cohen, who directs the influential Kids on the Block and Bridge Builders programs for Child and Family Services. With her husband, University of Tennessee law professor Neil Cohen, she has organized a group of Jewish volunteers who serve meals once a month at the Volunteer Ministry on South Gay Street. (As this area used to be the heart of Knoxville Jewish business, there is poetic as well as social justice in their project.) Rody Cohen also served as co-chair on the Knoxville Jewish Federation's social services committee, which cares for the community's Jewish aged and those in crisis.

The intriguing question of how this new, mostly northern professional population affected the social status of Jews in the South has not been studied in detail. Yet it seems clear that two major engines of change were in play: First, the new arrivals simply didn't have as much regard for the old southern social order. Second, the jobs they held and the institutions in which they worked were quickly rising in social status within the general community. "My own guess is that while race and religion were still the most important points of demarcation in the South, Jews were excluded from the in-group," Leonard Dinnerstein wrote to me recently in answer to a question about this subject. "Once Jews started moving into the universities and high tech firms, it was they who had no interest in associating with high-class Gentiles: they could take them or leave them. Once that happened, the Protestant elite realized they were no longer the social arbiters . . . they would have to make some accommodation if they wished to remain elite in the community. You can't be a member of an elite group if the most important people (and in this case it became the wealthy, the high tech and the university faculty) couldn't care less about what games you were playing—with or without them."

"Northern Jews who came south didn't have the same feeling of having to know one's place," agrees Bernie Bernstein. He noticed that many of these new Jewish arrivals were eagerly sought after at the highest social levels simply because they were educated, sophisticated, and entertaining. "For example, people were lining up to go to [psychology professor] Howard Pollio's lectures," he points out. As the economy of Knoxville began to increasingly revolve around the university and hospitals, so did its higher social life. Jews who held top-ranking positions were welcomed at elite parties, and their spouses were gradually invited into elite volunteer groups.

A look at newspaper headlines for the past ten years shows the prominence of local Jews—including many who stay quite active in Jewish community affairs. Dr. Mitch Goldman, chairman of the Department of Surgery, performs a kidney transplant on a seventeen-month-old baby girl, the youngest transplant recipient ever at the University of Tennessee Medical Center; Dr. Leon Bogartz is named medical director of St. Mary's Hospital; Dr. Robert Koppel, head of East Tennessee Children's Hospital, kicks off a major building expansion; Rosalind "Roz" Andrews retires after fifteen years as chief U.S. probation officer for East Tennessee; Knox County Criminal Court Judge Mary Beth Leibowitz presides over the sensational "Jobs Corps" murder trial; Janet Gurwitz, assistant district attorney, heads the new domestic violence unit; Marty Iroff becomes the drug and violence prevention specialist for the Knox County school system; Dr. Barbara Levin is named national rural health provider of the year; Barbara Bernstein serves a term as chairman of the Knoxville Museum of Art, an institution built in great part through the efforts of oncologist Dr. Alan Solomon, who chaired the building committee. When tensions flare between the African American community and local police, Bernard Bernstein is chosen by the mayor to head a blue ribbon panel to investigate and seek answers. The following year, when the University of Tennessee Medical Center is privatized, he is appointed its first chairman of the board of trustees.

Within the past two decades, several Knoxville–Oak Ridge rabbis have made notable contributions to the general community, as well as to national and international Jewish causes. Rabbi Noah Golinkin, who served Heska Amuna from 1969 to 1977, pioneered a groundbreaking adult Hebrew literacy program used all over the nation. On the local scene, Rabbi Mark Greenspan (Heska Amuna 1980–86) became a key figure on the board of Child and Family Services, an agency for abused and neglected children. He chaired a committee on adoptions of children with disabilities and acted as an informal chaplain to the staff and volunteers. In recognition of his many efforts, the Rabbi Mark Greenspan Therapeutic Play Center was dedicated in 1986. Rabbi Howard Simon of Temple Beth El (1986–99) took on the mission of helping to develop an Interfaith Clinic for the working poor in Knoxville. He was a member of the original planning board and served two terms as president. Simon became involved in several other civic affairs, including United Way and Leadership Knoxville, whose aim was to train the next generation of local leaders.

Perhaps the most unusual rabbi to ever serve in this area is Victor Rashkovsky, who was an art sociologist and film reviewer in Moscow before emigrating in 1973. Ten years later, when he was graduated from the Reform movement's Hebrew Union College–Jewish Institute of Religion, Victor Rashkovsky became the first émigré from the former Soviet Union to be ordained as a rabbi in either the Reform or Conservative movements. He came directly from the seminary to his current post at the Jewish Congregation of Oak Ridge, where he thrived in the congenial atmosphere of a small synagogue almost entirely filled with scientists and their families. The next year, Rashkovsky began to record a Russian-language program on Jewish topics for "Voice of America," which broadcast his tape in Eastern Europe. The weekly program, which discussed religious ritual and customs, historical events and ethical concepts, was taped in Victor's Oak Ridge home for fifteen years, finally concluding in 1999. The previous year, Rashkovsky made the first of two trips back to Moscow, funded by national Jewish organizations. On the first, he helped conduct four seders. (He and his wife, Avigail, who heads the religious school at Temple Beth El, usually conduct another Russian language seder each year for émigrés from the former Soviet Union who have settled in Knoxville and Oak Ridge.) I'm not sure whether this is another first, but Rabbi Rashkovsky is one of the few rabbis who "officially" celebrated becoming a bar mitzvah at age fifty, surrounded by a joyous group of congregants and friends. I remember it as one heck of a *simcha*.

Some years ago, a Heska Amuna rabbi who hailed from the northeast became upset by reports that a skinhead supremacist group was threatening violence in the area. "I was really worried and wondered if we should be making some kind of a public protest," he recalls. An influential community member quietly contacted him and promised "the matter would be taken care of," and so it was. "We wield a considerable amount of influence for our small numbers, but it's always done very, very quietly," says Arnold Schwarzbart. "There's a certain feeling of not wanting to rock the boat. It's just not the way people do things here."

Though the community still prefers not to assert itself as a Jewish political entity, it has gradually taken on structures that help get things done. According to historian Leonard Dinnerstein, most Jewish communities around the country founded Community Relations Committees in the 1930s and 1940s, when American anti-Semitism was at its height. The Knoxville community didn't form such a committee until the 1980s, after it had established the Knoxville Jewish Federation as its political-financial umbrella organization.

Today more than ever, KJF (which keeps its headquarters in the Arnstein Jewish Community Center and shares its executive director, Bernard Rosenblatt, with that organization) is the place where Temple Jew and Synagogue Jew cooperate. Numbered among KJF's many accomplishments is its work to create a chair of Judaic Studies at the University of Tennessee, currently filled by Dr. Gilya Gerda Schmidt. The chair is partially funded by the Jewish community and several private Jewish donors in the local area.

In many respects, Knoxville is a mirror of the Oak Ridge experience of the 1940s—and the later experiences of Jews in many university towns. Professionals settle here without family ties. They bond with each other around holidays, Jewish life-cycle events, carpooling to Hebrew school, and the volunteerism essential to educating their children as Jews. Many who never belonged to a temple or synagogue before affiliate in Knoxville because they crave the benefits of Jewish culture. Also, they seem to realize the importance of belonging to a religious group in this ardently churchgoing town. In that respect—just as Robinson and Tuchfeld noted thirty years ago—living in a sea of Baptists tends to create a pool of more committed

One of the most intriguing aspects of Knoxville Jewish life is the significant number of converts or "Jews by choice" who have taken on important roles in the community. In a time when the community has shifted from family-linked merchants to unrelated professionals, they are redefining the ethnic parameters of Jewish life. Nora Messing has been a Heska Amuna religious school teacher and community organizer for more than a decade. Courtesy of the Messing Family.

Jews. The tendency to hang together with a group and conform to its mores runs very deep in the South.

One of the most intriguing changes in the past thirty years has been the impact of intermarriage on the community. Here, as elsewhere, intermarriage has been a major factor in Jewish life. Nationally, it has been estimated that more than 50 percent of all first-time marriages are to non-Jews, and only a small percentage of these marriages result in the conversion to Judaism of the non-Jewish partner. However, in this community, "Jews by choice," as converted Jews are often called, have been heavily involved in Temple, Synagogue, Center, and Hadassah. Jews by choice have served as Sisterhood president, Temple president, and chairman of the Synagogue board of trustees. Kosher caterer Marilyn Burnett is a Jew by choice; so are the Synagogue's veteran religious school teachers Kathy Goodfriend and Nora Messing. For the record, Nora is the only African American member of the community. Upon conversion, she chose the Hebrew name "Zipporah," after the Kushite wife of Moses. Like Zipporah—and many other Jews by choice—she helped bring her spouse back to active Jewish observance. Nora's husband, Patrick, who was raised in the Synagogue but had drifted away from the Jewish community, now tutors Heska Amuna's bar and bat mitzvah classes in Torah trope, the ancient cantillation for reading Scripture during services. This year Nora headed the Jewish Family Living Program at Heska Amuna. In one of the most popular events she organized, dozens of parents and children gathered old photos and made posters of their own family trees, lining the Synagogue's walls with a dramatic illustration of how far the tribe has wandered and how much diversity it now contains.

What becomes evident in this blended community is that Jewishness is not just a religion or even an ethnicity, but rather a "peoplehood." Whether we are drawn into this tribal circle by birth, marriage, or choice, it is a multidimensional way of belonging, exactly that "complex network of filaments" that Robinson and Tuchfeld described thirty years ago. Even as the influx of outsiders has changed this community, the new arrivals have been changed and drawn into the web of local Jewish culture and responsibility.

Notes, February 29, 2000. Now the story arrives where it first began— in the private, unassuming little square of the New Jewish Cemetery. Sarah Green Robinson is being laid to rest on this warm sunny day in late winter, shortly before her ninety-second birthday. "When I die," she once said to me with her characteristic dash of vinegar, "I told my children to stick an onion in the handkerchief and make a good show of crying at the funeral, then go home and don't cry anymore. Because I lived a good, long life."

Sarah's large family had no need of onions that day as they crowded beneath the funeral canopy. She was survived by three of her original eight siblings, four children, eight grandchildren, ten great-grandchildren, and dozens of other relations. She spent the final months of her brief illness in her own home, surrounded by a gathering of kin who traveled from all over the country to say good-bye.

Many months before—already thinking ahead to the bat mitzvah ceremony planned for spring 2001—my twelve-year-old daughter, Anna, had asked Sarah if she would accept an *aliyah*, the honor of "going up" to say Torah blessings, which is usually given to family and close friends on such occasions. "Honey, I'm a little too Orthodox for that," smiled the woman who had once been the only girl in Vine

Street's basement Hebrew school of 1918. "I don't go up on the *bima*. But it makes me feel good that you asked."

A few weeks before the end, I took Anna to see her old friend, who had sat beside her in the Synagogue on so many Shabbats. Sarah held her hand in a frail grip, but the eyes were still strong and clear. Despite increasing weakness, she had even thought to give Anna a keepsake from her own things. It was a beautiful little gold bracelet, just right for a young girl. "This is a present for your bat mitzvah," Sarah told her. "I'm sorry I can't be there, but I know you'll be wonderful."

"I won't ever forget you," Anna told her. At home, the bracelet was put away like a secret promise, to be brought out again when Anna stands wrapped in her first *tallit*, on the day she becomes bat mitzvah. Her coming of age as a Jewish woman will be so different from that of her friend, born and raised in this same community just eight days less than eighty years before. Yet some patterns never change, and among them is the deep, mysterious power of the old to bless the future of the young.

Fall and winter, spring and summer. Birth, adulthood, marriage, death. Jewish life is a dance through time, encircled by those timeless rituals that give us each a place to stand and a way to be together. Today Anna stands in the cemetery, waiting her turn with family and friends to place three shovels of earth into Sarah's grave. I shiver to see my young one doing such a thing, but I also feel glad inside. Through simple acts like this, we comprehend the loss of treasured ones and bind ourselves to the dance of time, to the chain of our tradition. May it always be so in this small, obscure corner of world Jewry. *Ken y'hi ratzon*—So may it be. ∞

Knoxville/Oak Ridge Community Leaders

Jewish Community Center Presidents

M. B. Arnstein	(Honorary)
Jay Moskowitz	1930–31
Ben Winick	1931–32
Harry Goldberger	1934–35
Max Friedman	1935–37
Sam Herrmann	1937–38
Max Wolf	1938–40
C. B. Brown	1940–43
Dewey Reich	1945–46
Max Morrison	1946–47
Hymie Billig	1947–49
Louis Glazer	1949–50
D. B. Liberman	1950–52
Harold Winston	1952–54, 1969–70
David Blumberg	1954–56
George J. Busch	1956–58
Isadore Rosenblatt	1958–60
Herbert Nash	1960–62
Louis Joffe	1962–64
Emanuel Schenkel	1964–65
Sam Rosen	1966–67
Joseph Miller	1967–68
Theodore Reback	1970–72, 1978–80
Bernard Silverstein	1972–73
Barry Wolf	1973–75
Arnold Schwarzbart	1975–77
Gordon Brown	1977–78
Mark Harris	1980–82
Dolly Reback	1982–84

Arnold Elliott	1984–86
Judith Teasely	1986–88
Douglas Morrison	1988–89
Steve Oberman	1989–90
Stephen Hirschhaut	1990–91
Bart Brody	1991–93
Ernie Gross	1993–95
Karen Robinson	1995–97
David Oleshansky	1997–99
Ellen Schnoll	1999–

Knoxville Jewish Federation Presidents

Michael Feinman	1984–85
Mitchell Robinson	1986–87
Arnold Schwarzbart	1988–89
Barbara Bernstein	1990–91
Jeff Becker	1992–93
Ianne Koppel	1994–95
Mary Beth Leibowitz	1996–97
Mary Linda Schwarzbart	1998–99
Pace Robinson	2000–

Knoxville Chapter of Hadassah Presidents

Gertrude Weinstein	1927–28
Ida Siegel	1928–32
Ray David	1937–39
Mary Corkland	1939–41, 1942–44

(Mary Corkland founded Knoxville Young Judaea in 1933 and reorganized the Knoxville chapter of Hadassah in 1939, then serving as Honorary President for Life.)

Frances Klein	1944–45
Esther Rosen	1945–46, 1951–52
Bess Good	1952–54
Mary Brown	1954–55
Rae Davis	1955–57
Sylvia Cooper	1957–58
Marion Goodstein	1958–59, 1966–68
Sadie Miller	1959–61

Sylvia Silver	1961–64
Pearl Zwick	1964–66
Pessa Brody	1968–70
Advisory Council	1970–71, 1985–86
Marcie Silverstein	1971–73
Mary Linda Schwarzbart	1973–75
Elene (Lee) Miller	1975–77
Myra Corkland Weinstein	1977–79
Barbara Leeds	1979–81
Carol Harris	1981–83
Judy Balloff	1981–83
Carol Balloff Abeles	1986–88
Ianne Koppel	1988–90
Ellen Berez (Co-Pres.)	
Elaine Dobbs (Co-Pres.)	1990–92
Marian Jay	1992–94
Judith Kaufman	1994–96
Mary Ellen Schaefer	1996–98
Judy Megibow	1998–2000

Temple Beth El Presidents

The following names were taken from the 1957 dedication booklet and Temple files; there were some discrepancies on dates and name spellings between various sources, so I have used the oldest source in each case.

S. Bissinger	1868–69
Emanuel Samuel	1869–70
Frank Heart	1870–71
M. Heart	1872–73
Emanuel Samuel	1873–85
Sol Hyman	1886–87
Louis David	1888–89
Sol Hyman	1890–91
David Rosenthal	1891–92
Frank Heart	1892–93
Louis David	1895–96
L. Berwanger	1893–95
Emanuel Samuel	1896–98
Sol Hyman	1899–1900

Louis David	1901–2
Emanuel Samuel	1903–4
Isadore Beiler	1904–5
Louis David	1906–7
Emanuel Samuel	1908–11
I. Adler	1912–14
Frank Heart	1915–16
Isadore Beiler	1917–18
Alex Kleinberger	1918–19
Morris Deitch	1920–21
Jacob Reich	1922–23
Nathan Marks	1924–25
Jacob Reich	1926–27
Albert Levy	1927–28
Isadore Beiler	1929–30
Albert Levy	1930–31
Ben Jacobs	1931–32
Jay Moskowitz	1932–33
Edwin Deitch	1933–34
Clarence Strasburger	1934–38
Sam Herrman	1938–39
David Blumberg	1939–40
Maurice Konigsberg	1940–42
Clarence Strasburger	1942–44
Edwin Deitch	1944–47
Morris Reich	1947–48
Harry Davis	1948–50
Maurice Konigsberg	1950–52
Edward Reich	1952–54
Edwin Miller	1954–56
Melvin Goldberger	1956–57
Lester Popkin	1958–59
Harold Winston	1959–61
Dewey Reich	1961–63
Max Morrison	1963–65
Herbert Nash	1965–67
Bernard Silverstein	1967–69
C. Steven Lisser	1969–71
George Finer	1971–73
Eugene Zuckerman	1973–75

Marcus Bressler	1975–77
Henry Fribourg	1977–79
Harry Marx	1979–81
Clare Maisel	1981–82
Richard Hahn	1982–84
James Scheiner	1984–86
Harry Marx	1986–88
Richard Jacobstein	1988–90
Bob Freeman	1990–92
Charolette Evans	1992–94
Mike Cole	1994–96
Alan Smuckler	1996–97
Ann Wayburn	1997–99
Jeffrey Arbital	1999
Beverly Schultz	2000–

Temple Beth El Sisterhood/Women of Reform Judiasm Presidents

Fannie Burger	1877–79
Rosa Deitch	1914–16
Fanny Beiler	1925–27
Nettie Adler	1927–29
Sadie Samuel	1929–31
Jennie Levy	1931–33
Emilie Strasburger	1933–35
Helen Blaufeld	1935–37
Ada Averbuch	1937–38
Pauline Krieger	1938–40
Emilie Strasburger	1940–42
Rose Mark	1942–44
Elise Levy	1944–45
Ruby Bass	1945–46
Lillian Kern	1946–48
Blanche Jacobs	1948–50
Helen Blaufeld	1950–52
Bernice Finer	1952–53
Zelda Morrison	1953–54
Leona Popkin	1954–56
Clara Miller	1956–58

Sylvia Silver	1958–60
Marian Davis	1960–62
Bess Good	1962–63
Bette Margolin	1963–64
Marcia Silverstein	1964–66
Selene Spiegle	1966–67
Muriel Zuckerman	1967–69
Esther Joffe	1969–70
Zelda Morrison	1970–71
Bernice Finer	1971–71
Alexandria Rosen	1971–73
Donna Winston	1973–75
Sylvia Silver	1975–78
Wilma Weinbaum	1978–79
Linda Scheiner	1979–81
Elaine Freeman	1981–82
Terri Soss	1982–83
Mary Sampson	1983–85
Linda Scheiner	1985–87
Ellen Markman	1987–89
Mimi Brody	1989–91
Karen Smith	1991–93
Mimi Brody	1993–97
Beverly Schultz	1997–2000
Karen Smith	2000–

Heska Amuna Synagogue Presidents

B. J. Thorpe	1911–12
Max Finkelstein	1913–14
Morris Bart	1914–15, 1921–22
Lazar Schwartz	1915–20
A. G. Bart	1923–24
Morris B. Robinson	1924–25
B. Schiff	1927–29
Isadore Rosenblatt	1930–33, 1942–45, 1958–63
Jacob B. Corkland	1934–39, 1950–51, 1978–79
Max Friedman	1940–41

Joseph Epstein	1946–47
Rabbi A. J. Robinson	1948–49
Fred Millen	1952–55
Harry Caller	1956–57, 1964–67
Ruben Robinson	1968–69, 1982–83
Harold Diftler	1970–71
Theodore Reback	1972–73
Norbert Slovis	1974–75
Bernard Bernstein	1975–77
Jerrold Becker	1980–81
Arnold Cohen	1984–85
Michael Friedman	1986–87
William Berez	1988–89
Harold Leibowitz	1990–97
Marion Goodstein	1992–93
Arnold Schwarzbart	1994–96
Evan Ohriner	1996–97
Norbert Slovis	1998–present

Heska Amuna Synagogue Chairmen of the Board of Trustees

Max Wolf	1948–49
C. B. Brown	1950
Louis Glazer	1951–52, 1958
Joseph Epstein	1953
George Busch	1954–55
Miles Siegel	1956
Mitchell Robinson	1957, 1963–65
Harold Leibowitz	1959–60
David Liberman	1961–62
Bernard Bernstein	1966–67
Norbert Slovis	1968–69
Joseph Goodstein	1970–71
Sanford Weinstein	1972–73
Theodore Reback	1974–75
Leonard Miller	1976–77
Arnold Cohen	1978–79
Lawrence Leibowitz	1980–81
Ronald Isenberg	1982–85

William Berez	1984–85
Mark Harris	1986–87
Eugene Rosenberg	1988–89
Marilyn Liberman	1990–91
Gale Hedrick	1992–93
Manny Herz	1994–96
Michael Zemel	1996–97
Neil Feld	1998–99
Martin Iroff	2000–

Heska Amuna Sisterhood Presidents

Molly Chazen	1929–30
Rebecca Millen	1931–39
Rose B. Robinson	1940–43, 1945
Gertrude Roth	1944
Sarah Robinson	1946, 1951
Ann Kohler	1947
Jane Corkland Rosenblatt	1948
Kate G. Caller	1949
Regina Axelrod	1950
Rose W. Busch	1952
Florence Woolf	1953–54
Pearl Gitman Zwick	1955, 1956
Ann Seif	1957
Hannah Nius	1958–59
Mary Kaplan Brown	1961–63
Marilyn Slovis Cohen (Presser)	1964–66
Selma Smullian	1967
Natalie Robinson	1969–71
Marion Goodstein	1972–74
Alice Gerson Renert (Katcher)	1975–78
Marilyn Liberman	1979–81
Marcia Katz	1982–83, 1990–93
Fay Gluck	1984–87
Melissa Sturm	1988–89
Barbara Phelps	1994–96
Pat Rosenberg	1996–97
Dina Kramer	1998–2000

Jewish Congregation of Oak Ridge Presidents

William Bernstein	1944–45
Hyman Rossman	1946
Herman Roth	1947
William Elkin	1948
Sidney Miller	1949–50
Arnold Kitzes	1951–52
Gilbert Klein	1953–54
Joseph Spector	1955–56
Herman Roth	1956–57
Herbert Hoffman	1958–60, 1983, 1986–89
Myron Lundin	1961–62
Ernest Silver	1963–64, 1969, 1993–95
Marvin Kastenbaum	1964–65
Irwin Spewak	1965–68
Irving Barrack	1970
Seymour Levin	1971–72
Stanley Cantor	1973–74
Martin Ginsburg	1975–76
Roberta Steiner	1977–78
George Lawson	1979
Frances Silver	1980–81
Melvin Sturm	1982
Sig Mosko	1984–85, 1992
Murray Hanig	1990–91
Mira Kimmelman	1994–97
Al Good	1998–2000
James Bogard	2000–

Jewish Congregation of Oak Ridge Sisterhood Presidents

Molly Helfman	1944–48
Thelma Stiller	1948
Val Rossman	1949
Ruth Carey	1950
Molly Horn	1951
Ann Klein	1952
Eleanor Agron	1953

Evelyn Hanig	1954
Shirley Blumberg	1955
Teresa Schwartz	1956
Frances Silver	1957, 1968–70, 1998–91
Rose Holz	1958
Mildred Landay	1959–61
Betty Maskewitz	1961–63, 1987–89
Lil Zasler	1963–65
Vivian Jacobs	1965
Roslyn Breman	1966–68, 1981–82
Myra Hoffman	1970–72, 1991–93
Roberta Steiner	1972–74
Jeannette Gilbert	1974–76
Eileen Handler	1976–79, 2000–
Vera Maya	1979–81
Anne Greenbaum	1983–85
Faiza Solomon	1985–87
Rhonda Sternfels	1993–95
Catherine Braunstein	1996–98
Rosalie Nagler	1998–2000

Knoxville/Oak Ridge Rabbis

Heska Amuna Rabbis

A. Michaeloff	1890–91
N. Tagress	1891–95
Isaac Winick	1895–1922
J. Shapo	1922–24
A. J. Robinson	1924–26
Pincus Knobel	1926–29
Isaac Levine	1929–35
Jacob Holzman	1935–39
Leo Bergman	1939–40
Joseph Goldberg	1940–42
M. M. Goodman	1942–48
Myron Machenbaum	1948–49
Louis Cassel	1949–50
Bernard Rubinstein	1950–52
Jacob Kurland	1952–54
Aaron Mauskopf	1954–57
Morton Shalowitz	1957–60
Max Zucker	1960–69
Noah Golinkin	1969–77
Irving Margolies	1978–80
Mark Greenspan	1980–86
Yehoshua Kahane	1986–89
Arthur Weiner	1989–96
Shlomo Levine	1996–

Temple Beth El Rabbis

Jerome Mark	1922–25
Milton Greenwald	1928–31
Ephraim Rosenzweig	1932–34
Norbert Rosenthal	1934–38
Ralph Blumenthal	1938–39

Jerome Mark	1939–42
Luitpold Wallach	1944–47
Leo Stillpass	1947–50
Paul Liner	1950–51
Solomon Foster	1951–52
Meyer Marx	1952–63
Harold Ruebens	1963–69
Matthew Derby	1969–81
Paul Kaplan	1981–86
Howard Simon	1986–99
Beth L. Schwartz	1999–

Jewish Congregation of Oak Ridge Rabbis

From JCOR files.

Martin Kessler	1953–57
Kenneth Bromberg	1958–62
Alexander Gelberman	1964–67
Robert Marcus	1968–71
Daniel Zucker	1978–81
Victor Rashkovsky	1983–

Bibliographic *Essay*

1. Laying Down the Stones

*U*pon completion of this work, all notes, documents, and audio-tapes (except those which are borrowed from private individuals in the Knoxville Jewish community) will be placed on file in the Knoxville Jewish Federation's Archives of the Jewish Community of Knoxville and East Tennessee.

With regard to Knoxville's New Jewish Cemetery, many anecdotes came from Scott Hahn, longtime chairman of the Cemetery Committee for Heska Amuna Congregation. A list of Temple interments was provided by the chairman of Temple Beth El's Cemetery Committee, Dr. Henry Fribourg. An account of the rather ornate monument created by Morris Bart appears in *The Marble City: A Photographic Tour*, text by Jack Neely, photography by Aaron Jay (Knoxville: University of Tennessee Press, 1999).

For background on Jewish ritual, a useful all-round source was Rabbi Joseph Telushkin's *Jewish Literacy: The Most Important Things to Know About the Jewish Religion, Its People and Its History* (New York: William Morrow and Company, 1991).

Barbara Winick Bernstein's family files provided the letter from her father, attorney Ben Winick, written during the Scopes trial, as well as other early Knoxville Jewish correspondence. A major source for early East Tennessee Jewish history was documents found in the Knoxville Jewish Federation files, including deeds for the old and new cemeteries. A well-researched but unsigned local history pamphlet written for the

U.S. bicentennial supplied details of Alexander Cuming's grandiose plan to settle Jews in East Tennessee. The original source for that information was Bernard Postal and Lionel Koppman's *A Jewish Tourist's Guide to the U.S.*, with a foreword by Dr. Jacob Marcus (Philadelphia: Jewish Publication Society of America, 1954). A congregational history of Temple Beth El written by Anne Marcovitch in 1947 includes a mention of early-nineteenth-century settler Rabbi Abraham Ben Jaddai, which she attributes to research by the late archivist Dr. Jacob Marcus of Hebrew Union College. A mention of Solomon D. Jacobs, mayor of Knoxville in 1835, appears in a listing of past mayors as part of the Knoxville city directory, 1891–92.

Anne Marcovitch's history (included in the fortieth anniversary memorial book for Temple Beth El) and an even more extensive history written by Dr. Harold Winston for the Temple's centennial book in 1964 were basic sources of information. To trace the presence of early Jewish settlers, I also made use of Knoxville census rolls, city directories, obituary files, and cemetery records in the McClung Historical Collection of the Knox County Public Library (KCPL). Other details (verifiable through census and directory records) were available in a short historical pamphlet written by the late Temple Beth El Rabbi Matthew Derby as part of the U.S. bicentennial celebration in 1976.

A profile of Gen. Louis Gratz, who became mayor of North Knoxville, appears in Harry Golden and Martin Rywell's book of biographical sketches, *Jews in American History: Their Contribution to the United States of America* (Charlotte, N.C.: Henry Lewis Martin Co., 1950). A woodcut of Mayor Gratz also appears in the 1891–92 Knoxville city directory, and clippings about him were available in the KJF archives.

Details of the Gen. Ulysses S. Grant's abortive attempt to expel Jews from Tennessee with "General Orders Number 11" are recounted in Geoffrey Perret's biography *Ulysses S. Grant: Soldier and Politician* (New York: Random House, 1997).

2. Famous Sons

The Old Market House, which burned down in 1959, is pictured in the postcard album entitled *Knoxville, Tennessee*, by Elena Irish Zimmerman (Dover, N.H., and Charleston, S.C.: Arcadia Publishing, 1998) and in numerous photos owned by the Thompson Photo Archive, available at all Thompson Photo locations in Knoxville. Columns about Adolph Ochs are included in local historian Jack Neely's two collections entitled

Knoxville's Secret History (Knoxville: Scruffy City Press, 1995, 1999). Other details about the Ochs family came from two additional sources: Gerald W. Johnson, *An Honorable Titan: A Biographical Study of Adolph S. Ochs* (London and New York: Harper and Brothers, 1946), and an article by modern Ochs biographers Susan Tifft and Alex S. Jones, "The Family," *New Yorker* 65, no. 8 (April 19, 1991): 44–52. I also made use of city directories and clippings about the family found in KJF files. Information about Ochs's cousin Jacob Blaufeld was obtained from his descendant Maurice Schwarzenberg and city directories. Among many useful details, Richard Licht related to me that the cigar store run by Jacob's son Walter used to be the place to scalp University of Tennessee football tickets.

Several newspaper accounts of Max Arnstein's early exploits in Knoxville were in the KJF files and in Arnstein Jewish Community Center memorial books. Other information was provided by obituary files in the McClung Historical Collection of KCPL, cited above, as well as Temple Beth El Centennial and Arnstein Jewish Community Center fiftieth and seventy-fifth anniversary memorial books.

Another source of information about Jewish residents in the city around the turn of the century is *Knoxville Cookbook 1900*, a reediting of the original 1901 cookbook of the Knoxville Women's Building Association, produced by Frank T. Rogers in 1957. Within its pages are listings from the 1900 Knoxville city directory as well as much background material on the city at that point in history. Scott Hahn, who lent me this useful book, was kind enough to go through the directory and pick out the approximately forty-five identifiably Jewish families listed.

A good source of background information on Eastern European Jewish immigration to the United States is Roger Daniels, *Coming to America: A History of Immigration and Ethnicity in American Life* (New York: Harper Perennial, 1991). See page 223. Also quoted in this chapter is Eli Evans, *The Provincials: A Personal History of Jews in the South*, rev. ed. (New York: Simon & Schuster, 1997). An excellent source of statistical information and analysis of East European impact on small Southern Jewish communities is found in Lee Shai Weissbach's article "Eastern European Immigrants and the Image of Jews in the Small-Town South," in *American Jewish History* (Baltimore: Johns Hopkins University Press, 1997), 231–62. The Weissbach article makes references to the role of the Industrial Removal Office, also mentioned in *The Making of an Ethnic Middle-Class: Portland Jewry Over Five Generations* (Albany: State University of New York Press, 1982).

3. Temple Jews and Synagogue Jews

Information about the Lippner family was obtained from an audiotaped interview with Mary and Rose Kate Lippner made by Barbara Bernstein, as well as a later videotaped interview made by Harold Winston. Other information came from a newspaper interview with Fanny Stein Lippner in a *Knoxville Journal* article dated March 11, 1982. Miriam Reich Blumberg kindly provided details of her family's store, her father's membership in the Scottish Rite Masons, and early Temple Beth El picnics. A vivid portrait of Heska Amuna's basement Hebrew School of 1918 was drawn for me by Sarah Green Robinson, with additional details provided by an audiotaped interview of Dora and Ike Green made by Barbara Winick Bernstein in 1984. Anecdotes about the redoubtable Mrs. Fanny Beiler were provided by Richard Licht, who put together a rich and gossipy collection of stories told by his family.

Lee Shai Weissbach's study of Eastern European Jews in small southern towns, cited in chapter 2 notes above, was helpful in providing background about early Zionism in the South. Minutes of early Knoxville Hadassah meetings were kindly provided to me by Mary Linda Schwarzbart from her own files. The opposing anti-Zionist viewpoint and the impact of classical Reform Judaism was outlined well in Myron Berman, *Richmond's Jewry 1769–1976: Shabbat in Shockoe* (Charlottesville: University Press of Virginia, 1977), 206–35.

Useful insights on Reform Judaism were also found in Malcolm Stern's essay entitled "The Role of the Rabbi in the South," in *Turn to the South: Essays on Southern Jewry*, edited by Nathan M. Kaganoff and Melvin I. Urofsky (Charlottesville: University Press of Virginia for American Jewish Historical Society, 1979). This work also contains a specific reference to events in Knoxville. Background on the impact of "genteel anti-Semitism" was obtained from Leonard Dinnerstein, *Anti-Semitism in America* (New York and Oxford: Oxford University Press, 1994), as well as Dan A. Oren, *Joining the Club: A History of Jews and Yale* (New Haven: Yale University Press in cooperation with American Jewish Archives, 1985). Another source on the coming together of German and Eastern European Jewish factions in the South was Carolyn LeMaster, *A Corner of the Tapestry: A History of the Jewish Experience in Arkansas 1820s to 1990s* (Fayetteville: University of Arkansas Press, 1994), xxii.

The New York career of Knoxville native son Morton Deitch was detailed in the corporate biography by Jerome K. Lieberman, *Stroock, Stroock, and Lavan: An Informal History of the Early Years 1876–1950*. Ben

Bodne's story was told to me by Barbara Winick Bernstein. Frank Dryzer's brief history was included in an obituary on file in the KJF archives.

4. Family Affairs

Almost all of the stories contained in this chapter were obtained from oral interviews with living community members or from interviews on audiotape made by Barbara Winick Bernstein and friends during the 1980s. One notable exception is a well-documented family history written by Genevieve Shaw Kramer, which is quoted at length in the text. Information about changes in urban Knoxville—including the impact of closing public saloons in 1907 and major land annexations in 1917— were obtained from the article "Time Pieces" by Jack Neely (*MetroPulse*, June 24, 1999, 9–14). Background on the Leo Frank lynching was obtained from Leonard Dinnerstein, *The Leo Frank Case* (New York and London: Columbia University Press, 1968). Knoxville population estimates here and elsewhere in the text were obtained from city directories and official sources researched for me by the very helpful staff at the McClung Historical Collection of Knox County Public Library. The story of how Lou Balloff once helped Campbell County lawyer Roy Asbury was reported in the Knoxville *News Sentinel*, July 3, 1994.

5. Business and Politics

Knoxville city directories in the McClung Historical Collection were used to establish the addresses of Jewish merchants in 1949. Other important sources of detail for this chapter were issues of the *Center Menorah* and Hadassah directories on file in the KJF archives. Census data from the Jewish Community was published in the *Center Menorah*. Rabbi Howard Simon of Temple Beth El (retired) found photos and scripts from the 1947 Beth El historical pageant on file in the Temple library. Leonard Dinnerstein's *Anti-Semitism in America*, cited above, was helpful in establishing the course of Southern Jewish anti-Semitism in the postwar period. For an example of how this pattern changed in smaller towns, I made use of an intriguing article by Deborah R. Weiner at the University of West Virginia, "The Jews of Keystone: Life in a Multi-Cultural Boomtown," *Southern Jewish History* 2 (1999): 1–23. Details about the life of jeweler-politician Max Friedman were obtained from McClung Historical Collection obituary files and interviews with his relatives. Obituary files were also used to chart the life of Adrian Burnett. Most information about David Blumberg was obtained from an audiotaped interview done by Barbara Winick Bernstein.

Many of the accounts of early Oak Ridge life were originally published in fortieth and fiftieth anniversary books compiled by members
of the Jewish Congregation of Oak Ridge. Other memories by the
late journalist Ruth Carey are found in a book of essays entitled *These
Are Our Voices*, edited by James Overholt (Oak Ridge, Tenn.: Children's
Museum of Oak Ridge, 1987). Facts about the life of clothier Sam Miller
came from an essay written by his granddaughter Melissa Miller of Knoxville. The anecdote about Arthur Hays Sulzberger and anti-Zionism is
obtained from the Tifft-Jones article on the Ochs family referenced in
chapter 2, above. The report of David Ben Gurion's visit to Knoxville is
reported in *The Southern Israelite*, May 11, 1951, 1, and in the *Center
Menorah* in September 1951.

6. The Good Old Days

The dedication booklets produced by Temple Beth El, Heska Amuna
Synagogue, and Arnstein Jewish Community Center to commemorate
the opening of new buildings were a major source of information for this
chapter. Both booklets are on file at the KJF archives. Back issues of the
Center Menorah also provided detail, including Jewish community census
information. Hadassah directories also provided useful information about
Jewish residential and business life. Background about that venerable
1950s institution the Sisterhood Interfaith Tea appeared in the history
In Pursuit of the Tree of Life by Belinda and Richard Gergel (Columbia,
S.C.: Tree of Life Congregation, 1996). Dinnerstein's *Anti-Semitism
in America*, cited above, was also useful in establishing the regional
context, as were e-mail comments from *Southern Jewish History* editor
Dr. Mark Bauman of Atlanta Metropolitan College. Comments by Rabbi
Kenneth Bromberg appeared in Jewish Congregation of Oak Ridge's
fiftieth anniversary booklet. Details of Mira Kimmelman's Oak Ridge
experience came from oral interviews, as did background on the career
of Knoxville attorney Bernard E. Bernstein.

7. A Snapshot of Changing Times

The primary source for this chapter was the master's thesis "A Study of
Communality in the Jewish Community of Knoxville, Tennessee," by
Shmuel Robinson and Barry S. Tuchfeld (University of Tennessee, 1972).
My copy came from the library at Heska Amuna Synagogue. To estab-
lish the regional context, Lee Shai Weissbach's study of small southern
Jewish communities, cited above, was extremely helpful. Background

on the growth of the University of Tennessee was obtained from *To Foster Knowledge: A History of the University of Tennessee 1794–1970* by James Riley Montgomery, Stanley J. Folmsbee, and Lee Seifert Greene (Knoxville: University of Tennessee Press, 1984) as well as *Tennesseans and Their History* by Paul H. Bergeron, Stephen V. Ash, and Jeanette Keith (Knoxville: University of Tennessee Press, 1999). A similar pattern that links growth of Jewish population to university expansion is found in North Carolina's Raleigh/Durham/Chapel Hill area, reported on by historian Dr. Leonard Rogoff in "Synagogue and Jewish Church," *Southern Jewish History* 1 (1998). His upcoming book on the subject is *Homelands: Southern Jewish Identity in Durham and Chapel Hill, North Carolina* (Tuscaloosa: University of Alabama Press, 2001).

8. Inside Out and Outside In

Religious school population numbers were supplied by Temple Beth El and Heska Amuna records. Overall population numbers were estimated for me by KJF Executive Director Bernard Rosenblatt from address files. Comparison population numbers from 1941 were derived from the *American Jewish Yearbook*, supplemented by other sources, such as the 1948 census done locally. The percentage of non-southern Jews currently living in the South was taken from correspondence with Dr. Leonard Dinnerstein, who used census and other records for his estimate. Statistics on intermarriage were obtained from the article "How many children will stay Jewish?" by Eliyahu Salpeter, published in *Ha'Aretz*, August 31, 1999. ∞

$\mathcal{I}$ndex

A Separate Circle was designed and typeset on a Macintosh computer system using PageMaker software. The text is set in Janson, and the chapter openings are set in Nuptial. This book was designed by Cheryl Carrington, typeset by Kimberly Scarbrough, and manufactured by Thomson-Shore, Inc. The paper used in this book is designed for an effective life of at least three hundred years.